T0188504

FOOD STORAGE

FOR SELF-SUFFICIENCY AND SURVIVAL

FOOD STORAGE

FOR SELF-SUFFICIENCY AND SURVIVAL

THE ESSENTIAL GUIDE FOR FAMILY PREPAREDNESS

ANGELA PASKETT

CONTENTS

CHAPTER 1

Disasters can strike at any moment, so it's important to have a ready supply of food on hand. The kit described in this chapter is designed to be portable so you can use it during an evacuation, but also if you are stuck at home without access to grocery stores.

CHAPTER 2

Food storage can help you through a widespread disaster, but it can also help you through personal financial difficulties by reducing your grocery bill during tight times. This chapter helps you identify which foods you should store based on your personal preferences and how much you should keep on hand.

CHAPTER 3

While large-scale disasters are rare, they could happen. Plus, long-term food storage helps you beat inflation—you can eat food a year from now that was purchased at today's prices. You can also stock up on foods in season and during sales to take advantage of even lower prices.

continued

APPENDIX

INTRODUCTION

The seeds of my own food storage journey were planted as a child. I grew up with a mother who canned garden produce, milked goats, cooked from scratch, and built bookshelves using boards and wheat cans. When I started a family of my own, storing food got serious. The responsibility my husband and I faced as parents—to provide for ourselves and the children who blessed our lives—became a driving force. I did not want to be dependent on a grocery store or government agency to feed my family if there were an emergency. Storing food just made sense.

So I set out to build my food storage. There were few resources at that time, but I learned as much as I could about which foods to store, how to store them, and how to use them from the limited books, seminars, and classes that were available. Most important, I actually started storing food. I tested what I learned from those seminars and books in my own life and with my own family. There has been a lot of learning and more than a few mistakes along the way. But with each can of food I put away, I felt that much more peace about my family's ability to provide for ourselves.

I've never had to use my food storage for a large disaster. I did not personally experience any of the devastating natural disasters in the recent past like Hurricanes Katrina, Ike, or Sandy. I haven't even had to live through a power outage that has lasted longer than two days. So has storing food been a waste of time and resources? Absolutely not. What I found is that storing food is so much more than an emergency plan. It is a means by which my family can be self-sufficient every day of the year, regardless of whether we have to deal with an emergency situation or not.

Food storage has helped me stretch my family's income in tight budget months, pack quick meals for short-notice trips to the mountains, and create healthy meals for my family without constant trips to the grocery store. And that food is there for us in the event we do experience a long-term emergency, whether that is a power outage, natural disaster, or a personal emergency such as illness or job loss.

About five years ago, a friend of mine asked for help getting started with her food storage, and thinking I could help her and maybe a few other friends and family members, I started the blog, **foodstorageandsurvival.com**, Food Storage and Survival. My handful of readers has grown to a worldwide audience. I now host a weekly radio show as well as teach seminars and classes on food storage and family preparedness. I have been blessed to be able to help many more than just my one friend, and I want to help you, too.

WHAT'S IN THIS BOOK?

I did not write this book to tell you the single best way to store food for your family. I don't believe there is one best way. Each of us has our own unique circumstances, and our food storage will reflect that. Age, family size, health concerns, income, and living conditions will all factor into your personal food storage plan. Within each chapter are a variety of options including options for preserving food, packaging food, and getting various foods in your storage plan. You will find some options will work for you and some won't. Those that don't work for you may be perfect for someone else.

This is also not a cookbook or a complete survival manual. This is an in-depth, nuts-and-bolts guide for storing food. The first three chapters cover storing food for portable emergency kits, short-term storage, and long-term storage. Water storage and filtration are next, then canning, drying, freezing, and packaging your own food storage. I give options for purchasing food for storage and detail a variety of foods that are available to store. Sustainable food storage, including raising livestock, gardening, and hunting, is also covered as a means of providing ongoing food sources for your family. And we wind up with proper storage techniques, ideas for places to store your food, and how to use food storage to make your own favorite recipes. And, of course, there are worksheets throughout the book to help you plan, purchase, and rotate your food storage. With the information in this, book you can build and carry out your personal food storage plan to fit the needs of your family.

With all the uncertainty in the world, there is peace in preparing. I want that peace for you. Thank you for letting me help you along your own food storage journey. Now, let's get started.

1. FOOD FOR 72-HOUR EMERGENCY KITS

You're enjoying an average lazy morning at home, reading stories to the kids. Suddenly, you feel a rumbling. The ground lurches and there is a sickening groan. You grab the kids and drop to the ground. Glass breaks, books fall to the ground, and the lights flicker off. Then, as quickly as the tumult began, it's over. In an instant, the day has changed, including your plans for dinner. You were going to go to the grocery store to pick up the makings for tonight's dinner, and now the roads are damaged and the power is out. There won't be any shopping today. Maybe not for a few days. What do you have to feed your family?

The idea of having a supply of food on hand for emergency use just makes sense. Even government agencies like the Federal Emergency Management Agency (FEMA) and state public safety agencies recommend having at least three days of nonperishable food ready. Combine that three-day emergency food supply with some other emergency supplies, put it all in a container that can be grabbed quickly in the event of a disaster, and you have a 72-hour kit. A 72-hour kit is also commonly referred to as an emergency kit or a bug out bag. The kit described in this chapter is for use at home or during an evacuation, and we don't want to limit ourselves to seventy-two hours, so we'll use the term *emergency kit*. An emergency kit is best when designed to be portable so it can go with you in the event you need to evacuate your home. It can also be used if you are sheltering in place at your home or workplace.

BEFORE YOU PACK

There are a number of options for foods that are easily packed in an emergency kit. Each has its pros and cons, and the choice that is best for your kit may not work for someone else. In fact, you may find that the food that works best for your kit now may not meet your needs five years from now if your dietary needs change. The primary considerations when packing emergency kit foods are:

- calorie count
- flavor
- ease of preparation
- shelf life
- weight

Calorie Count

Calories equal energy. They are the fuel that keeps your body running. You don't want to fill your emergency kit with foods that will do little to sustain your energy level. Life will not be normal following an emergency. You may be working harder than usual doing cleanup or other manual labor, or you may need to evacuate your home entirely and travel to a safer location on foot. You will almost certainly be under increased stress levels. You do not want now to be the time you start cutting calories. In fact, following an emergency, you are probably going to need to increase your daily calorie count above your normal level to make up for the added physical strain.

Flavor

You want food in your emergency kit that you and your family members will enjoy eating. Maybe you've heard someone say something like, "In an emergency, you'll eat any food you can get." While that may be true, the reason I'm packing a kit for my family and myself is so I'm not forced to take what anyone else is offering. Right now, before an emergency, I have a choice of which foods I put in my emergency kit, and I prefer to stock foods that taste decent to me. The packaging may make a pre-packaged meal looks really tasty, but those photos are no guarantee that it will actually look like that, or taste how you imagined, when it is actually prepared. While it does add to the expense of stocking your kit, I highly recommend testing every food included in your emergency kit to see if they are foods that you will enjoy eating. This is especially important if you have children.

Ease of Preparation

Some emergency kit foods, such as jerky or granola bars, are ready to eat right out of the package and don't need to be heated. Other foods, such as canned meals and Meals Ready to Eat (MREs), don't need to be heated but would sure taste better warm. Freeze-dried or dehydrated meals will need some preparation. I'll cover some methods of cooking that can be included in an emergency kit later in this chapter. As you are deciding what to put in your kit, you need to consider whether you will have the ability or desire to heat foods or if you just want something you can open and eat.

Shelf Life

Many foods packed specifically for emergency use are designed to have a shelf life of up to ten years if stored properly. Other foods will have much shorter shelf lives (some under twelve months) and will need to be rotated frequently. If you are organized enough to rotate the contents of your emergency kit regularly, you will have no problem storing any of the foods I will discuss. If, however, you want to put your kit together and forget about it for a while, you'll want to use the longer shelf life foods. Shelf life of any foods in your kit will be affected by where and how your kit is stored. If your kit is exposed to moisture, light, and wide temperature fluctuations, the stated shelf life of your emergency foods will decrease.

Weight

Three days of food can be heavy. In addition to all the other contents of your emergency kit, your food and water can easily make your kit too heavy to carry. Not many of us are champion weight lifters, or even in what might be considered great physical condition. Age, injuries, illness, physical condition, or other special situations like pregnancy or disabilities are all factors in the amount of weight an individual is able to carry. Weight is less of a consideration if you will be staying in your home with your kit or traveling by vehicle.

TYPES OF FOOD FOR EMERGENCY KITS

There are a number of options for emergency kit foods.

Grocery Store Foods

Although specialty retailers offer many foods specifically designed for use in emergencies, you can purchase plenty of foods for your emergency kit at your local grocery store. Grocery store foods that are great for an emergency kit include:

- canned soups and pastas
- tuna and crackers
- cups of noodles
- beef jerky

- granola bars
- dried fruits and nuts
- candy or other snacks

Pros: These foods are generally inexpensive, and if they are a part of your regular everyday diet, you know you will be willing to eat them in an emergency. Your family will be familiar with the flavors and textures of the foods.

Cons: These foods tend to have the shortest shelf lives of all the foods you could include in your kit, so if you use them, make sure to rotate your kit foods regularly. One way to do this is to restock the kits in the spring and use the old food for your first road trip or camping trip of the summer. Grocery store foods are also not packaged for "packing." Metal cans take up more space in your kit than meals packed in flexible packs and bags. Add a manual can opener to your kit if your cans don't have easy-opening tabs.

MREs

MRE stands for Meal Ready to Eat. These are precooked meals that are packed in flexible heavy plastic packaging. MREs were originally created for military use, but are now readily available from nonmilitary retailers. They can be purchased as complete meals or in individual meal components, allowing you to pick and choose what parts of the meal you want to include in your kit.

Pros: MREs have a shelf life of up to five years. All of the food in an MRE has been fully cooked, so it doesn't need to be heated before eating, although with the available MRE heaters, heating your MRE takes about 3½ oz. (100mL) of water, and heat could add immeasurably to the palatability of the meal. These meals are high in calories and salt content and are designed to be eaten during stressful periods. MREs are ready to eat, and no additional water is needed to hydrate the meal.

Cons: MREs are heavy and bulky for a portable kit. For flavor, MREs are my least favorite emergency food. Try some out before you buy cases of them.

Survival Bars

Survival bars are the food most commonly included in commercially assembled emergency kits. These bars are produced by companies like S.O.S. Food Lab, Mainstay, and Datrex and are one of the least expensive, most compact ways to get a lot of calories in your kit. A 2,400-calorie survival bar costs between four and five dollars at the time of this printing and weighs about 1 pound (454g).

Some of these bars taste better than others, so again, I'd do a taste test with your family if you are planning on using these in your kit. I found I liked

Contents of an MRE   **Variety of survival bars**

Homemade Survival Bars

You can use food storage ingredients to make your own homemade survival bars. One batch provides approximately 2,000 calories, and they have a very long shelf life. I have had one of these bars in my car for more than five years.

Ingredients:

- 2 cups oats (quick or old fashioned)
- 2½ cups powdered milk
- 1 cup sugar
- 3 tbsp. honey
- 1 3-oz. package flavored gelatin powder (orange or lemon are best—this recipe is sweet)
- 3 tbsp. water

Instructions:

1. Mix the oats, powdered milk, and sugar together in a heat-resistant bowl.
2. In a medium pan mix water, gelatin powder, and honey. Stirring constantly, bring the mixture to a boil and remove from heat.
3. Add boiled mixture to dry ingredients. Mix well. It will be very dry and somewhat difficult to mix together. If the dough is too dry to mix, add a small amount of water a teaspoon at a time. You want this dry, so be careful not to add too much water.

the flavor of the Mainstay bars and have included some in our kits for a high-calorie breakfast option, but have other foods for lunch and dinner. Some friends who also tasted the bars liked one of the other brands better.

Pros: These bars don't need to be cooked and are easy to eat on the go. They are also small and cost-effective. You can get an entire day's worth of calories (2,400) in one bar that costs less than five dollars.

Cons: While the bars will meet your caloric needs, they are not as filling or as comforting as a traditional meal and don't offer a lot of variety for flavor. If all you have are survival bars, you will survive, but you may never feel you had your appetite satisfied.

4. Shape the dough. You can shape it into a single loaf about the size of a brick or press firmly into a parchment-lined 9" × 13" (23cm × 33cm) pan and cut into individual bars prior to drying.
5. Place on a cookie sheet and dry in the oven at low heat, 200°F to 250°F (93°C to 121°C), until thoroughly dry (1½ to 2 hours). You could also dry the bars in a food dehydrator at 145°F for 4–5 hours.
6. When your bars are cool, wrap them in aluminum foil or seal in a vacuum sealer bag or Mylar bag to store.

These bars are a little more bulky for the calorie count than the commercial bars. You can eat the bars dry or cook them in water.

Want to change up the recipe? Try some of these variations:
- Use different flavors of gelatin powder or leave it out altogether.
- Add flavored extracts such as vanilla, almond, or raspberry.
- Crush up a vitamin C tablet in your powdered ingredients.
- Add protein powder as a portion of the powdered milk.
- Use powdered soy or goat milk for the powdered milk.
- Use molasses instead of honey.
- Add dried fruits or nuts (adding these will decrease shelf life).

These alterations may have a small effect on the end calorie count, shelf life, or nutrient content.

Freeze-Dried or Dehydrated Meals

Many food storage and backpacking companies make freeze-dried and dehydrated meals that can be used in an emergency kit. You'll find quite a variety of meal flavors available, and the preparation methods and flavor quality vary a great deal depending on the brand. Some of these meals require boiling the entire meal for fifteen to twenty minutes, which will use a lot of fuel. Others can be prepared by bringing water to a boil and then adding the boiling water to the food and letting it sit. This method requires less fuel consumption.

Pros: These meals are extremely lightweight and easy to pack in your kit.

Cons: They require water for rehydration. This means you will need to pack extra water for them or have some method of purifying water from a natural source. You will also need to pack some means of heating the water and possibly a metal container in which to heat the food. We will discuss various ways to cook your emergency kit foods a little later in this chapter.

You can also make your own dehydrated or freeze-dried meal mixes as an alternative to purchasing the commercial meals. There are some cookbooks available that have recipes for dry meals. I recommend *The Meals in a Jar Handbook* by Stephanie Petersen. Or you can convert some of your favorite family recipes to use dry ingredients, seal all the ingredients together in a Mylar bag, and pack those in your kit. Information on converting recipes can be found in chapter eleven of this book, and how to pack food in Mylar bags is covered in chapter six.

EXTRAS

Meals may be your main focus during an emergency, but a few extras can improve morale at mealtime or in between. Here are a few extras to add to your kits.

- Candy. Hard candies have a long shelf life when stored away from moisture. You can also store chocolate, but it should be rotated more frequently.
- Seasonings. Little salt or pepper packets, packets of ketchup, salsa, etc. can help the flavor of your emergency kit foods. These can be purchased at warehouse stores or restaurant supply stores.
- Hydration mixes or flavor additives for water. Pack individual servings the size of a sugar packet or a small bottle of concentrated flavor designed for water. These don't take up much space and can improve the hydration you receive from your water and improve the flavor, especially if you are using chemicals such as iodine to treat your water.

- Protein or nutrition bars such as PowerBars or Clif Bars.
- Packets of freeze-dried fruits or yogurt bites for snacking.

You may find that your kit will contain multiple types of food items. In fact, this is a good idea. It is impossible to predict exactly what your circumstances will be after a disaster. Will you be staying where you are, driving out, or hiking out? Will there be time to cook? Will you end up needing to feed someone with food restrictions? Packing a variety of foods gives you options.

PACKING FOR THE LITTLE ONES
Food for Children

Children are a special consideration when packing emergency kit food. For the most part, they can eat the same foods as the adults; however, children tend to be more choosy than adults when it comes to food flavors and textures, so a can of their favorite pasta meal may be much more welcome than some unfamiliar MRE that they don't like the taste of.

In my family, there are varieties of freeze-dried meals my kids will eat and some they won't touch. So if you have children you are preparing an emergency kit for, be sure to run a taste test of the foods before you pack. Take the foods you are planning to store on a camping trip or a picnic at the park and see if your kids like the flavor enough to actually eat them.

Food for Babies

The ideal source of food for young infants is a nursing mother. This is also the best option for packing as it takes no extra space, is always clean and the perfect temperature, and replenishes itself regularly. However, even a baby who is

Watch the Weight

Packing for children adds bulk to your emergency kit. They can usually pack some of their own food in their individual kits, but depending on their age and physical ability, they may not be able to carry a full three days' worth of food on their own. You may need to carry your child, your kit, and your child's kit when you leave your house. Not many people are physically able to get very far packing that kind of weight, so consider using other methods of transport to help haul the load. Strollers, bike trailers, and wagons are all options you likely have on hand if you are unable to use a vehicle.

nursed 100 percent of the time in normal, everyday life should have formula packed in his emergency kit. If the mother is not with the child at the time of the emergency, or if she were to sustain some kind of serious injury or even die, that baby still needs to eat. Powdered formulas come in cans or in individually measured packets. It generally has a shelf life of over a year. Make sure you also include a bottle in your kit, and either pack or have means of obtaining enough clean water to mix the formula.

Babies four months and older can eat solid foods. Dry infant cereal mixes are available from most baby food manufacturers and are a filling, inexpensive, and easy food to pack in an infant's emergency kit. You can reduce bulk by pouring the cereal out of the box and into a zipper-seal bag, then sealing the bag in a vacuum sealer bag or Mylar bag to help it stay fresh.

Some manufacturers now package baby foods in pouches instead of the traditional glass jars. This type of container works very well for packing in an emergency kit. You can also make your own powdered baby foods for your infant's emergency kit. Vegetables such carrots, sweet potatoes, and squash work very well. Steam or boil the vegetable until it is soft, then puree it into a paste and spread it on food dehydrator trays as you would fruit leather. After thoroughly drying the puree, chip it off the trays and use a blender to break it into

Cooking on a Dakota Fire Hole

You can build your own "stove" in the ground by making a Dakota Fire Hole.

1. Dig a small hole vertically into the ground—up to 12 inches (30cm) in diameter and 12–15 inches (30–38cm) deep. Save the sod from the top of your hole to replace it when you're done using your fire hole. This larger hole is where your fire will be.
2. About 8 inches (20cm) from your original hole, dig another hole about 6 inches (15cm) in diameter. As you dig, angle this second hole toward the bottom of your original hole so you are creating a tunnel between the two holes. You can work from each end of the tunnel to make digging it easier. This tunnel will create a draft and feed air to your fire.
3. Build your fire in the larger hole. You can place a grill or metal rods across the top of your hole to hold your cooking pot.

The Dakota Fire Hole is also a great option when building a fire in windy conditions and when you want a fire at night but don't want the light to expose your location.

powder. To use the food, simply add water to the powder (warm water works best), stir, and let the powder rehydrate into a pureed baby food. Freeze-dried fruits and vegetables can also be blended or crushed into a powder to be used as baby food powder. If you will be including dehydrated baby foods, make sure your infant kit contains a bowl and spoon for the mixing and feeding.

As your baby gets older, you will be able to use many of the foods you are packing for the adults and/or older children in your family. Pasta meals like macaroni, spaghetti, and stroganoff are especially well suited to older babies' eating abilities. Freeze-dried foods also add a wide variety to what can be packed for older babies. Most babies can easily eat freeze-dried potato dices, corn, mangoes, berries, and yogurt pieces dry once they are eight months old or older.

COOKING YOUR EMERGENCY KIT FOODS

Many of the foods you may consider having in your emergency kit will require some method of cooking. You don't want to stock your kit with freeze-dried meals and then have no way of heating water. Thankfully, there are many ways to cook emergency kit foods.

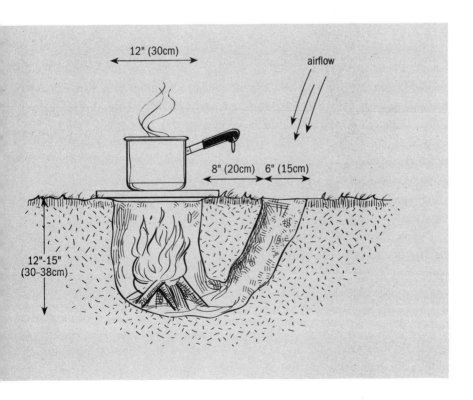

Firebox folding biomass stove   **Solo Stove biomass stove**

Fire

Cooking over an open fire is one of the most basic methods. Because fire-starting equipment (ignition source, tinder, and accelerants) is already a part of a well-stocked emergency kit, this method only requires that you add a fire-resistant pot, pan, or metal cup to hold the items you want to heat. Bringing water to a boil over an open fire can require a lot of fuel. You will need to source lots of firewood from your surroundings and have a steady supply on hand every time you cook.

Pros: Requires little extra equipment—only fire-starting material and a basic cookpot or metal cup.

Cons: You must have access to an adequate amount of firewood or other material that you can safely burn and cook over. It will take time and energy to collect the fuel, and you often don't have a lot of either during an emergency.

Biomass Stoves

Biomass stoves are a step up from cooking over an open fire.

Pros: These stoves require no specific fuel to be carried because they burn biomass—sticks, grasses, and other naturally occurring combustibles.

Cons: Because these stoves are made to be compact, each one has a limit to the size of wood that can be fed into it. They are not like a campfire that eventually can be fed a large log that will burn for a while. To keep your fire going and your food cooking in a portable biomass stove, you will need to watch the fire and feed it frequently. One of the more expensive stove options, they range in price from sixty-five to one hundred dollars.

These stoves come in various sizes and designs, the following being some of the different brands available in a portable size.

Kelly Kettle Trekker biomass stove

Canister and liquid fuel backpacking stoves

Firebox: The Firebox is a biomass stove that folds flat when not in use, so it is smaller to pack than some of the other stoves. It is built so you can easily place a pot or cup on top of the fire, but it is sturdy enough to support larger pots as well.

Solo Stove: The Solo Stove is another small biomass stove made specifically for backpacking. It is a round stove smaller than the open Firebox, about the size of a large mug. It has a vented design that intensifies the heat in the cooking chamber.

Kelly Kettle: The Kelly Kettle is a biomass stove that can heat water and cook food at the same time. This kettle is designed as a double-walled chimney, with the water filling the space between the two walls and the fire burning up through the center. With the pot support inserted in the top of the kettle, you can cook on the top of the chimney while heating your water in the chimney walls. It is an extremely efficient design for heating water and food using very little fuel. At approximately 12 inches (30cm) high and 4 inches (10cm) in diameter, it is one of the bulkier stoves to pack.

Backpacking Stoves

A small backpacking stove is also a good option for heating your emergency foods. There are many brands of backpacking stoves that are lightweight and easily packed. They operate similar to a gas-burning stove top. They can fold up very small and are very lightweight, but you also must pack adequate amounts of fuel for your stove. The fuel containers can be bulky. Backpacking stoves come in two varieties categorized by the type of fuel they use—canister stoves and liquid fuel stoves.

Alcohol stove; use either yellow bottle Heet or denatured alcohol as fuel.

Solid fuel Esbit stove

Kindle Cook flameless heater

Canister stoves are like small stove-top burners. They are designed to screw onto a compatible fuel canister and are usually less expensive and easier to operate than their liquid fuel counterparts.

Liquid fuel stoves have a detached, refillable fuel tank. All liquid fuel stoves can burn white gas, which is a purified gas product with no additives sold under brand names like Coleman Fuel and MSR SuperFuel. Many liquid fuel stoves can also burn less clean fuels like diesel, kerosene, and unleaded auto fuel. Liquid fuel stoves are a little more complicated to use, require more maintenance, and tend to be more expensive than the canister stoves, but they do offer the versatility of using multiple fuels and the ability to refill an empty fuel tank.

Pros: Backpacking stoves are made to travel, so are lightweight and take up little space. Canister fuel stoves can cost as little as fifteen dollars.

Cons: These stoves require specific fuels that need to be safely stored and packed prior to using.

Alcohol Stoves

Alcohol stoves burn denatured alcohol, which can be purchased at paint stores or online. Heet brand gas-line antifreeze in the yellow bottle (available in most auto parts stores) is an alternative fuel for these stoves. Light the alcohol with a match or spark from a striker-style fire starter. At around fifteen dollars, these stoves are also one of the least expensive options.

Alcohol stoves, like the Mini Trangia or Esbit alcohol stoves, are extremely small and lightweight. One of these stoves and its fuel can be carried inside a large metal mug, making these one of the most compact stoves you could include in your emergency kit. Due to their compact design, alcohol stoves do not have a place to rest your pot. You can create a makeshift pot rest by surrounding the stove with three rocks of the same height and resting your pot on the rocks. Most alcohol stoves also can be used inside either the Solo Stove or the Firebox brand biomass stoves, making your alcohol stove the fuel source instead of wood or other natural combustibles.

Pros: Inexpensive, small, and lightweight.

Cons: Alcohol stoves burn denatured alcohol, which must be safely stored and packed prior to using.

Solid Fuel Stoves

Solid fuel stoves burn fuel tablets, and most designs are extremely small and lightweight. Some come as a flat, die-cut piece of metal that can be bent into a stove shape when it is needed. Esbit is the primary manufacturer of solid fuel stoves and the fuel tablets used in them.

Pros: Very inexpensive, some cost less than ten dollars. Stoves and fuel tablets are both lightweight.

Cons: Built to burn only solid fuel cubes, which burn for approximately thirteen minutes each, so you'll need a stock of them for extended use. Durability is lacking in some models. Fuel tablets emit an unpleasant odor in storage.

Flameless Heaters

So far, all the cooking options I have covered require making a flame of some kind. There are also meal-heating options that don't require any kind of flame. MREs come with a heater specifically designed for use with the MRE meal. This heater is in a plastic sleeve that is slightly larger than the MRE meal pouch. The sleeve contains a chemical that heats up when it is combined with water. Add water and the unopened MRE meal component to the sleeve, and in five to ten minutes you have a heated meal.

The Kindle Cook Kit uses the same heating technology as an MRE heater. It consists of a rectangular stainless steel pot fitted inside a slightly larger hard plastic case that includes an airtight snap-on lid. Place a special cook pouch (made with the same chemical component of an MRE heater) in the bottom of the plastic case and add water. Then fill the stainless pot with the food or water you want to heat and place it in the plastic case. Snap on the lid and let it heat. The outer plastic case has a neoprene sleeve that makes it cool enough to touch or place on a tent floor without melting the floor while the cook kit is heating. This is a convenient kit for heating your food, but the cook pouches are single use, so you'll need to pack one pouch for each meal you want to heat. This can add some bulk to your emergency kit if this is your only cooking option.

Pros: These heaters can safely be used indoors and can also be moved while heating. No fire involved.

Cons: Heater packets are somewhat bulky, and the amount of food you can cook with each packet is limited to what will fit in the included pot. Each meal will need a separate packet to heat it, so the costs can add up. No ability to stir while cooking.

Non-stove Options

If you've ever left crayons or chocolate in your car on a hot day, you know solar power can get things pretty hot. Food or water placed on a vehicle dashboard facing the sun will heat up nicely. This isn't a quick option. It may take a couple of hours.

Also consider other places that produce heat like an engine or a metal roof in the sun. I've heard of one hiker using the source of a hot spring to heat his food and water, and another person who wrapped her food in foil and buried it in an active compost pile. Both are creative ways to get a hot lunch!

WATER FOR YOUR EMERGENCY KIT

Having clean water available after a disaster can prevent dehydration, disease, and even death. Experts recommend storing 1 gallon (4L) of water per day per person for drinking, cooking, and washing. If you are planning on evacuating your house with your 72-hour emergency kit, that would mean storing 3 gallons (11L) of water per person in your kit. A family of four would be carrying almost 100 pounds (45kg) of water! For this reason, most emergency kits that are meant for temporary use are actually packed with less water than recommended.

You have two main options for having water available in your emergency kit—either pack water or pack a method that will make found water sources safe to drink. I use a combination of both in my emergency kit.

Water Storage Options

Bottled water. You can purchase bottled water at most grocery and convenience stores. It's a readily available and inexpensive source of water for an emergency kit. It's convenient because you can drink a little at a time and put the lid back on after each drink. If you find your water tastes flat or stale, simply pour the water back and forth between two containers a few times or pour the water through a fine mesh cloth. This adds oxygen back into the water and can give it a better taste.

Water cartons and pouches. You can also find water specifically packaged for emergency kits. Aqua Blox packages water for emergencies in small cartons, very similar to juice boxes. You can also find individual serving pouches of water from companies like Datrex and Mayday. These emergency water options have an advertised shelf life of up to five years. The containers are opaque and airtight, preventing light and air from affecting the water. They also have an inner liner that keeps the water tasting fresher longer. The drawback to

Prefilter Found Water

Whether you use a water filter, a water purification method, or a combination of both, the treatment method will be most effective when the water you are treating is clear and free of visible particles and debris such as leaves, bark, or heavy sediment. You may need to prefilter found water by pouring it through a clean piece of fabric (such as a bandana, shirt, or sock) to remove large debris before you treat it.

storing these individual serving pouches is that once the package is opened, there's no way to reseal it, so you need to consume all of the water at once or empty the excess into a refillable water bottle.

Old soda bottles. You can wash empty two-liter soda bottles, fill them with water, and store them in your emergency kit. If you use this method, consider rotating the water every six to twelve months to prevent bacteria and germs from growing in the unsealed water. These bottles hold more than the smaller 20 oz. or 500mL bottles, but they are also more difficult to transport as they are large and heavy.

WATER FILTERS FOR EMERGENCY KITS

A portable water filter can provide a large quantity of clean water if you are near a source of water, such as a pond, creek, or even a rain barrel. These filters are a great way to increase the amount of clean water you can have available to you in an emergency. Most are lightweight and easy to pack. They come in a variety of styles.

Each of these filters will have a specific number of gallons or liters that it is capable of effectively filtering. They also have different pore sizes and filtering abilities. Even though a pump filter is kind of pricey (ranging from eighty to three hundred dollars), it may be a better option for you than the less expensive straw filter, depending on the number of people for whom you are planning on providing water and the number of gallons or liters you anticipate

Filtering vs. Purification

Filtering water means the water passes through some type of physical barrier. Water filters will eliminate particulate matter from the water, even removing bacteria and protozoa. A commercial filter is considered to be sufficient water treatment in the United States and Canada even though they do not rid the water of viruses.

Purifying water, usually through chemical or UV light treatment, removes the danger from bacteria, protozoa, and viruses. Purifiers are recommended for water treatment outside of the United States and Canada where the risk of viral infection is greater.

For the most complete water treatment, combine a purifier and a filter. Some commercial filters are also purifiers, using microfiltration in combination with a chemical treatment.

filtering. If you have a family, one pump filter could actually be less expensive than outfitting each individual with a straw filter or water bottle filter.

Hand Pump Filters

Hand pump filters have two hoses—one that sucks water from the source and one that outputs drinkable water. You draw the handle up to pull in the water. Then you push the handle down to force the water through a carbon or ceramic filter element and out the other hose. The clean water hose lets you pump the water directly into a cup, water bottle, or other container.

The filter has extremely small pores that allow water molecules through but block larger impurities including protozoa and bacteria. A few quality compact hand pump filters are the MSR Miniworks and the Katadyn Hiker Pro.

Water Bottles With Built-in Filters

Some water bottles have built-in filters that are attached below the mouthpiece of the bottle. To use, fill the bottle with untreated water (being careful not to splash the mouthpiece with the dirty water) and screw on the lid. The water passes through the filter by being sucked out of the bottle by the drinker. If the bottle is made of flexible plastic, the water can also be passed through the filter by squeezing the bottle and squirting the water out of the mouthpiece. These filters are easy to use, and if you are using one of the flexible bottles, you can squeeze the water into a cup or other container and use for cooking or hygiene. Seychelle and Berkey both make excellent flexible-sided water bottle filters.

Water Filter Straws

Water filter straws are the smallest and lightest weight filters available. To filter water, the user inserts one end of the straw into the water source and sucks it through the filter. These filters are also the least expensive filter option. Some, such as the LifeStraw, cost under twenty dollars. The drawback to straw filters is the water goes directly into your mouth. So they are a great way to get drinking water, but if you want to use the water for cooking or some other purpose, such as hydrating your baby food or mixing a bottle of formula, these won't work. They also require more suction power than a regular straw, so I recommend another type of filter for children under age five.

WATER PURIFICATION METHODS FOR EMERGENCY KITS
Water Purification Tablets

Water purification tablets (also known as iodine tablets) work by breaking down the cell walls of microorganisms in the water, rendering them inactive

Suggested Items for a 72-Hour Emergency Kit

- ☐ Water filter
- ☐ Water purification tablets
- ☐ Bottled water
- ☐ Food: MREs, freeze-dried meals, survival food bars, candy
- ☐ Fire-starting supplies: matches, lighter, striker, char cloth, fire-starting helps like WetFire or cotton balls soaked in petroleum jelly
- ☐ Flashlight, headlamp
- ☐ Light sticks
- ☐ Solar/crank radio
- ☐ Two-way radios
- ☐ Firearm and ammunition
- ☐ Knife
- ☐ Multi tool
- ☐ Rope or paracord
- ☐ Fishing line, hooks
- ☐ Change of clothes including footwear
- ☐ Poncho, emergency blanket, and/or large trash bag
- ☐ Compass

and making the water safe to drink. One tablet treats 16 ounces (500ml) of water. Dissolve the tablet in the water and wait twenty to thirty minutes before drinking. These tablets are very small and weigh almost nothing. They are also inexpensive and easy to find at any camping supply store. You can purchase water bottles marked with liquid measurements (both ounces and milliliters). Be sure to clean the mouth and threads of your water bottle with treated water before drinking from it. Contaminated water may have splashed out when you filled the bottle.

- ☐ Whistle, signal mirror
- ☐ Pencil, paper, deck of cards
- ☐ First aid kit
- ☐ Hand sanitizer
- ☐ Sunblock
- ☐ Insect repellent
- ☐ Hand warmers
- ☐ Leather gloves
- ☐ Toiletries: soap, contact solution and case, backup glasses, toothbrush/paste, etc.
- ☐ Toilet paper
- ☐ Feminine hygiene products
- ☐ Sewing kit
- ☐ Empty gallon-sized zip-seal plastic bags for repacking wet or soiled items
- ☐ Important documents on a thumb drive
- ☐ Small scriptures
- ☐ Cash (small bills/change)

Boiling Water

Although you've probably heard you need to boil your water to make it safe to drink, the water actually only has to reach 149°F (65°C), which is below boiling temperature, to be safe to drink. Boiling is used as a visual indicator that the water has reached a temperature high enough to be pasteurized. Boil your water using any of the cooking methods previously discussed. Feel free to boil your water as long as you like, but if it has reached boiling temperature, it is safe to drink—after it cools off, of course!

UV Purifiers

UV purifiers like those made by SteriPEN are one of the lesser-known portable water purification methods. They are light-weight and available in a wide-range of prices. Maybe the process of UV purification is perfectly clear to all you microbiologists out there, but this has always been one of the more mysterious water treatment options to me. You just swish this little light stick in your water and suddenly it's safe to drink? It sounds a little suspicious, but it works. UV light is the purification method used in most commercial bottling plants and in hospitals and water treatment plants. The super-short UV light waves produced by the purifier disrupt the DNA of all the microbes in the water, making them unable to reproduce and make you sick. UV purifiers are most effective in clear water, so if you're going to use one of these, you don't want to use it on murky water. A good prefilter or allowing the sediment to settle to the bottom and removing the top portion of the water are good ways to clarify murky water and make it clear enough to treat with a UV purifier.

EXPANDING PAST SEVENTY-TWO HOURS

If you have watched any coverage of the recent major natural disasters, you know it can take far longer than seventy-two hours before help arrives. Sometimes help does not reach very hard-hit areas for seven days or longer. Will a kit built to last seventy-two hours provide enough food and water to get your family through until help arrives or you are able to make it to a safer location? Make your kit into a seven-day kit or fourteen-day kit by adding more food. These foods can be included in your kit if you have room. Or you can fill a tote or backpack with extra meals and have it ready to grab on the way out of the house or available to use if you end up weathering the emergency in your home.

2. FOOD FOR SHORT-TERM EMERGENCIES: TWO WEEKS TO THREE MONTHS

Short-term food storage is a food supply that will feed your family for two weeks to three months in the event you are unable to purchase food. When you are starting to store food, the process can seem a little overwhelming. What do you need in your short-term food storage? Which foods should you store and how much should you keep on hand? How can you know what you need for three months if you can hardly get a list together for your weekly shopping trip? If you are asking these questions, you are not alone. Questions like these are actually quite common, and this chapter will address all of them. But let's start by exploring the benefits of having short-term food storage in your home.

WHY SHORT-TERM FOOD STORAGE?

There are many reasons you would want to have extra food on hand to feed your family for a longer period of time than a portable emergency kit could cover.

Large-Scale Disasters

Events such as a major natural disaster or long-term power outage in a region disrupt the entire food distribution system for grocery stores, and an average store can be cleaned out of the necessities in a matter of hours. In the event of a large-scale disaster, you don't want to be a part of the crowd rushing to the store to try to buy whatever is left on the shelves! They may be taking only cash payments or may not be open for business at all. Having a supply of food in your home means you can stay put where it is safe in the wake of a disaster and know you have what you need to get by until things get restored to normal.

Personal Finance Emergencies

While widespread disasters happen on a regular basis, the most common short-term emergencies, especially in a slow economy, are related to your own personal financial situation. Events like a job loss, pay reduction, or other financial strain can constitute an emergency in your family by making it difficult to keep food on the table. A long-term illness could have the same effect. But these types of emergencies don't cause widespread devastation. There will be no news coverage and nobody sending aid. You will be reliant only on what you have, and your family will still need to eat. If you have a supply of food on hand, you can temporarily take the grocery budget out of your expenses and still be able to feed your family.

Flexible Budgeting

Being able to remove the grocery budget from the monthly expenses can be helpful even if you don't incur a pay reduction. The most common times my family uses our food storage is when we are faced with a sudden extra expense like a large doctor or dentist bill or unexpected car repairs. We eat from our food storage and free up the grocery money to cover the new expense. And sometimes we choose to eat from our food storage so we save the grocery money and use it to purchase something we want, like to have gas money to drive to Grandma's or for buying something special. December is almost always a month in which we eat out of our food storage so we have extra cash for Christmas gifts. Having food storage allows us to occasionally manipulate our income to pay for other things we need. Just remember to restock the foods you use when your expenses get back to normal.

Saving Time and Money

Having a supply of food on hand will also reduce the number of trips you make to the grocery store, which will save you time and money. How many times have you had to run to the store for a single item you're out of but need for dinner? If you have food stored, you can save yourself the trip to the store and just go get that item from your food storage instead. Having food storage is like having a store in your own home that you can use whenever you need it.

SHORT-TERM FOOD STORAGE METHODS

There are a number of different ways to determine which foods and how much you want to have in your short-term food storage. For simplicity, we're going to use a three-month supply in all the examples in this chapter, but feel free to scale it down to whatever length of time you are planning to store food. We'll start with the most specific method.

THE MENU METHOD

One way to figure out what you need for a short-term food supply is to start with what your family eats on a regular basis and build your supply using the

Shelf-Stable Fresh Foods

For a short-term food supply, many items that are considered fresh produce can be kept in cold storage without electricity for at least three months. Most root crops and hard fruits keep well enough that they can be included in your short-term food storage plan. Consider foods such as:

- apples
- carrots
- turnips
- winter squash (acorn, butternut, etc.)
- potatoes
- sweet potatoes
- onions

foods you already eat. When you use menus, you can create a very detailed list of items to store in your short-term food storage. Here's how to use the Menu Method.

1. Write down your favorite meals. Keep track of the meals you make that your family likes to eat. Remember there are more meals in a day than just dinner, so be sure to include breakfasts and lunches in your list as well as any side dishes and snacks. The more meals you have in your arsenal, the more variety you'll have in your food storage, so try to gather as many as you can.

2. Determine if each recipe can be made with shelf-stable ingredients or ingredients that can be kept in the freezer or cold storage for at least three months. (Planning on using foods from your freezer in your short-term storage will work as long as you have power. It is best to have a backup plan for those meals in case your emergency involves the extended loss of electricity.) These are the recipes you will use for the Menu Method. Can you substitute or omit any fresh ingredients to make a favorite recipe food-storage friendly? Be creative so you can include variety.

3. Make an ingredient list for each recipe you will be using. Don't forget to figure in spices and seasonings as well as the amount of water the recipe uses.

4. Figure out how many times you will be making that recipe during the length of time for which you are setting up food storage. If you have 10 dinner recipes, the easiest calculation for 90 days (3 months) is each recipe will be used 9 times. If you have 15 recipes, each would be used 6 times, etc. However, you may like some recipes more than others, so feel free to customize the number of times you will make each one. Just be sure the total number of meals you buy for equals 270 (that's 3 meals a day for 90 days—a three-month supply). You'll need 90 days' worth of breakfast, 90 days' worth of lunch, and 90 days' worth of dinner.

5. Multiply the ingredient list by the number of times you will be making that meal to figure out how much you need to buy to stock your short-term food storage. Here's an example: One of the recipes in my menu plan is pancakes. One pancake meal requires 2 cups of dry pancake mix. I plan to have pancakes 9 times over the next three months, so I will need 18 cups of pancake mix in my short-term food storage. To complete this recipe I will also need to calculate how much water is needed to make the mix and the amount of syrup needed to cover them.

The Menu Method has two benefits:
1. It's easy to ensure you are storing an adequate amount of each food item.
2. You know you can use the foods in your storage to make meals that your family will not only eat but enjoy.

When circumstances require you to use your short-term food storage, chances are you will be under a little extra stress anyway. Being able to eat familiar meals during this time will decrease the emotional impact of the situation and maintain a sense of normalcy for your entire family even if circumstances have changed.

Here's a full example of the Menu Method so you can see how it works. First, I made a list of all my favorite meals, then narrowed that list down to those that can be made with shelf-stable ingredients, ensuring I had a written recipe that included measurements for each meal. Those recipes were then inserted in my short-term food storage planning chart.

After I determined how many times I will be cooking each recipe, I calculated the ingredients I will need to purchase. The Menu Method Planning Sheet in the appendix makes it easy to list and calculate all the ingredients.

Sample Master Menu List

BREAKFAST	
NUMBER OF TIMES RECIPE WILL BE USED	**RECIPE**
10	oatmeal
20	pancakes
10	dry cereal with powdered milk
10	muffins
10	cinnamon rolls
10	waffles
10	bacon and eggs with toast
10	biscuits and gravy
Total: 90 days of breakfast	

LUNCH	
NUMBER OF TIMES RECIPE WILL BE USED	**RECIPE**
10	macaroni and cheese
15	peanut butter and jelly/honey sandwiches
10	ramen noodles
10	tuna sandwiches
15	chicken quesadillas
15	canned pasta
15	canned soup
Total: 90 days of lunch	

DINNER	
NUMBER OF TIMES RECIPE WILL BE USED	**RECIPE**
7	Italian chicken
6	chicken and rice
7	chili
6	potato soup
6	clam chowder
7	beef stew
6	chicken noodle soup
7	stroganoff
6	tuna noodle casserole
6	shepherd's pie
7	enchiladas
6	fajitas
7	stir-fry
6	scalloped potatoes and ham
Total: 90 days of dinner	

Sides

Some dinner recipes won't require any side dishes, while others will need sides to balance the nutrition, add variety, and provide enough calories. Think about what sides you normally serve with each main dish and plan accordingly.

GRAINS	
NUMBER OF TIMES SIDE WILL BE USED	GRAIN
27	rice white, brown, flavored
30	bread or rolls
7	cornbread
Total: 64 days of grains	

VEGETABLES	
NUMBER OF TIMES SIDE WILL BE USED	VEGETABLE
13	green beans
13	peas
13	mixed veggies
13	corn
13	asparagus
13	spinach
12	carrots
Total: 90 days of vegetables	

POTATOES	
NUMBER OF TIMES SIDE WILL BE USED	POTATOES
5	baked
5	scalloped
5	mashed
5	fried
Total: 20 days of potatoes	

FRUIT (CANNED)	
NUMBER OF TIMES SIDE WILL BE USED	FRUIT
18	peaches
18	pears
18	fruit cocktail
18	pineapple
18	mandarin oranges
Total: 90 days of fruit	

SNACKS	
NUMBER OF DAYS SNACK WILL BE USED	SNACK
15	cookies
10	brownies
5	cake
18	crackers
18	fruit snacks
12	dried fruit
12	nuts
Total: 90 days of snacks	

After I got my recipes figured out, the next step was to determine how many times I wanted to fix each one. You can divide the days evenly between the recipes or make more of the foods you prefer (either for taste or ease of preparation!). My family really likes pancakes, so we'll have that more often than oatmeal, but for dinner I want to space the meals out evenly, so I'm just going to divide the meals equally. Make sure each column adds up to the number of days you will be storing food for. In this example, I'm calculating food for 90 days.

Fast Foods

Just because you're living off your food storage doesn't mean you need to make every meal from scratch. There will be times when you don't have the desire or the time to cook a meal from scratch. In good times, you can call and order a pizza or Chinese takeout, but in times of emergency, fast food from a restaurant won't be an option. Be sure your food storage plan includes some meals that are convenient and fast to cook. Canned meals like

Dry meal ingredients pre-assembled in a jar

chili, soups, and pastas that are made to heat and eat are a great addition to your food storage for times when you need or want fast meal prep.

You can also store all the ingredients for specific quick meals together in one paper bag or on one area of your shelf for quick preparation. If the meal can be made from all freeze-dried or dehydrated ingredients, you can premeasure the ingredients for one meal into a Mylar bag or mason jar and seal it with an oxygen absorber. These quick meals are then ready for anyone in the family to cook a delicious meal at a moment's notice. Remember to fool-proof home-mixed meals by including the cooking instructions so anyone can prepare them!

I continued this multiplication with the other meals in my plan to determine my master food list. As you create your master food list, you will find some ingredients repeat between recipes. In my example, I have potatoes as a side dish, and I will also have potatoes in my recipes for potato soup, clam chowder, beef stew, and scalloped potatoes and ham. When my shopping list is done, I will have all those individual amounts combined into one total amount of potatoes I need to have on hand.

The benefit of using the Menu Method is that the step of figuring out what you are going to eat from your food storage has already been taken care of before you actually need to use it. Because this is a short-term emergency plan, the meals can use foods that don't have extremely long shelf lives, like

Menu Method Planning Sheet, Example

Recipe Name: Italian Chicken (from **myfoodstoragecookbook.com**)

Number of servings in single batch: 8

Number of times recipe will be served: 6

SINGLE BATCH QUANTITY X NUMBER OF TIMES RECIPE WILL BE SERVED	QUANTITY USED TO MAKE A SINGLE BATCH	INGREDIENT
6	1	(16-oz.) box farfalle pasta
6	1	(14-oz.) can chicken broth
6	1	(10–15-oz.) can chicken
6	1	(4-oz.) can mushrooms
6–12	1	can diced Italian-style tomatoes (2 cans if you like it more saucy)
3 cups	½ cup	Parmesan cheese
6 tsp.	1 tsp.	Italian seasoning
6 tsp.	1 tsp.	garlic powder
6 tbsp.	1 tbsp.	dried parsley

Download a printable version of this worksheet at **www.livingreadyonline.com/foodstorage**.

raw potatoes. In order to make the best use of the foods you have purchased, it is wise to incorporate your storage recipes into your regular meals even when there is no emergency. Just be sure to restock what you use so you'll always have a supply of food on hand.

INVENTORY METHOD

The Inventory Method is another way to determine the contents of your short-term food storage. With this method, start by going through all your food cupboards, your refrigerator and freezer, and your deep freezer, and write down every food item you have on hand. You may need to do this shortly after you

Managing Leftovers

While leftovers make a great lunch for the following day during normal circumstances, in an emergency where there is no power and you don't have the luxury of refrigeration, leftover food is wasted food. Leftovers that aren't properly stored can cause food poisoning and serious illness if they are eaten after sitting at room temperature (or warmer in the summer) for too long. If you are in a power-out situation with no way to properly cool and store leftovers, consider halving large recipes or making smaller batches to keep from having leftovers at all.

make a trip to the grocery, or take inventory two to three different times over the course of a month to be sure you have all the regular foods included. Include meal items, condiments, snacks, everything. Be sure to write the date you are taking the inventory on the top of the list.

Keep the inventory list on your refrigerator or with your grocery list and note the date you run out of each item. From your list, you can figure out what you need to purchase by determining how quickly you use each item. Another easy way to track how long it takes your family to use up a multiple-use product (such as a bottle of ketchup) is to use a permanent marker to write the date on a package when you open it. Then record the date you finished using it on your inventory list. Use the inventory list in this book (download printable copies at **www.livingreadyonline.com/foodstorage**) to keep a paper record, or create a spreadsheet to record your results. For example, if one bottle of ketchup lasts two months in your house, you'll want two bottles of ketchup in your short-term food storage to ensure you have a three-month supply.

For items that get used quickly (such as a favorite snack or loaf of bread), keep a tally chart to figure approximately how many you use for a specified time period, and that number can be multiplied out to your goal storage amount. For example, if three meals in a week each use one can of peaches, then you need three cans per week or thirty-six cans for a three-month supply. Things that are used less frequently could be tallied over a month's time. Incidentally, this method also works great for nonfood items like cleaners and toiletries. Your chart will end up looking something like the following Food Inventory List.

Food Inventory List

Date of Inventory: July 1

FOOD QUICKLY EATEN		
FOOD	NUMBER CONSUMED IN 1 MONTH (USE TALLY MARKS)	NUMBER NEEDED (3-MO. SUPPLY)
Canned peaches	12	36
Canned chicken	8	24
Potatoes (in pounds)	20	60

MULTI-USE FOOD (E.G. CONDIMENTS, SPICES)			
FOOD	DATE FOOD WAS OPENED	DATE FOOD WAS USED UP	NUMBER NEEDED (3-MO. SUPPLY)
Peanut butter (18 oz.)	Sept. 5	Oct. 17 (6 weeks)	2
Shortening can	July 1	Sept. 1 (2 months)	2
Ketchup (50 oz.)	March 1	July 1 (6 months)	1

Round Up to Account for All Meals

With the Inventory Method, rounding up is the rule. In typical day-to-day life, it's unlikely that you eat every single meal at home. Your children might purchase lunch from the school cafeteria many days a week, and your family might go out to eat or pick up fast food for a meal on a weekly basis. All of the meals you eat outside of the home affect how much food is used in your house. If your family eats a lot of meals away from your house, increase your inventory numbers accordingly. In an emergency, you'll likely be eating every meal at home.

SUGGESTED AMOUNTS

If you're still unsure of how much food you need to store, you could determine what foods you need to store by using a chart of suggested food storage amounts (see the sidebar). These lists rarely encompass all the items you would want to have, but they do provide a guideline for assembling your storage.

PURCHASING COMMERCIAL FOOD PACKAGES

Some companies offer prepackaged foods that are advertised to last two weeks to three months or more. These come in two types—ingredient-based packages and meal-based packages. Ingredient-based packages will have a variety of different foods in the pack, and each individual food item is packaged in its own can. So you will receive separate cans of corn, beans, wheat, rice, pasta, peaches, or whatever is in the specific variety pack. Be aware that these ingredients are not customized to your family's eating habits, so you will probably end up with some foods that will be harder for you to use than others. These packages are a good starting point if you simply want to have a variety of foods on hand, but they may need some adjustment to better suit your personal situation and

Suggested Amounts for Three-Month Food Supply for One Person

Grains (rice, pasta, flour, cereal, wheat, oats): 75 lbs. (34kg)

Legumes (beans, lentils): 15 lbs. (7kg)

Fats and oils (cooking oil, shortening): 6 lbs. (3kg)

Dairy (powdered milk, evaporated milk, cheeses): 19 lbs. (9kg)

Sugars (sugar, brown and powdered sugar, honey, drink mixes, jams, and jellies): 15 lbs. (7kg)

Fruits (canned, dried, juices): 46 lbs. (21kg)

Vegetables (canned, dried): 46 lbs. (21kg)

Cooking essentials: baking powder, baking soda, vinegar, yeast, salt

Adapted from the Church of Jesus Christ of Latter-day Saints' *Essentials of Home Production & Storage* book.

Food Storage to the Rescue

Disasters happen to everyday people. Scott and his wife got caught in a storm that resulted in their power being out for twenty days! They found that food in a refrigerator doesn't last more than a few days when there is no power. They used their barbeque grill to boil water and cook simple meals from their stored shelf-stable food. They used water from their pool to wash themselves and flush their toilets. This experience taught Scott's family what they needed to survive without power. Years later, when Hurricane Sandy left them without power for six days, they were ready to be self-sufficient.

In another example, Heather experienced a terrible winter storm in her area that left most residents without power. Her food storage and other preparations allowed her and her husband to care for their family of three and open their home to host three additional adults and two children for a few days until power was restored. They had stored fuel for propane heat, oil lamps, powerless cooking options, and plenty of food storage. Heather was even able to accommodate a neighbor child's gluten allergy.

tastes. The packages are also assembled based on calorie count, not by recipe or meal. Putting the foods together into actual meals will be up to you.

Meal-based packages include a variety of premixed freeze-dried or dehydrated meals. Some also include a few freeze-dried ingredients that can be used as side dishes. These meal packages are designed for ease of preparation. I don't recommend purchasing a long-term food storage plan that consists primarily of freeze-dried entrees for a number of reasons. First, each plan has a limited variety of meals, and most of the meals have similar textures or "mouth feel." Variety is very important in any food storage plan because you may be eating the food for a long period of time. Second, you may not like the flavor of the meals. For example, if you get ten different meal options, maybe you like seven of them, and your kids will only willingly eat four of them. There could be too much salt, too little seasoning, a strange flavor to the sauce, or the flavor could be so rich that you don't want to eat enough of the meal to get full. Yet you are stuck with those meals you don't want as part of the package. This ends up as wasted food and wasted money. A third reason against using only meal-based food packages for your food storage is serving size. Most food companies use the industry standard serving size, which is probably smaller than what you are used to eating. I have found that if I want to feed four people from a freeze-dried entrée that is labeled as having four servings, the four people need to be myself and three of my small children. If you're planning to feed four adults with a four-serving entrée, they will all be able to eat, but they will probably still be hungry after they each had their share and the food is gone. While I don't think an extended food storage plan should consist entirely of freeze-dried meals, they might have a place in your plan. Having a few prepackaged meals that you have tested for flavor and serving sizes with your own family could make a good meal if you are in a situation that requires something fast and easy.

SUMMARY

To assemble your short-term food storage, you can stick to only one of the methods outlined in this chapter, or mix and match the methods to help meet your specific needs. Whatever method you decide to use to start your short-

Food Storage: Your Own Financial Aid

When Jane's husband was laid off from his job, they had nothing. They were barely making enough to get by before, and now unemployment wasn't even covering their house payment, much less food and clothing. They weren't eligible for food stamps, so they had nowhere to turn for food until they were earning money again.

But prior to the layoff, Jane had started storing food. They were able to live off of what they had put away in their pantry for two-and-a-half long months before a new job and new paycheck kicked in. Jane used the change out of their rainy-day fund jar to purchase fresh vegetables and meats on sale, and a few sundry items along the way, but almost all of what they ate during those months came from their food storage.

In another real-life example, Cheryl's husband took a job in another state that required him to live away from home and travel home on weekends. Because Cheryl had been storing food, they were able to free up part of their income to pay for his apartment in the town in which he was working.

After her divorce, Cheryl needed to rely even more on her food storage to get through a winter of unemployment and the following months of part-time and seasonal employment as she worked to provide for herself.

term food storage supply, the most important thing is simply to get started. You don't have to do it all at once. Start by selecting and purchasing one extra week of food, then build to two weeks, then longer. Having a well-rounded supply of food on hand to sustain your family for two weeks to three months will help you be more self-reliant every day and make you better prepared for most personal and regional emergencies. Ready for more? Let's explore long-term food storage.

3. FOOD FOR LONG-TERM EMERGENCIES: THREE MONTHS OR LONGER

Once you have established a short-term food supply, you are ready to branch out to long-term food storage. A long-term food supply will feed your family for three months or longer. As with a short-term food supply, long-term food storage will most likely be used for a personal emergency. Extended illness, job loss, or pay reduction can easily last longer than a couple of months. If you have inadequate income for a long period of time, you can still feed your family if you have food stored.

A long-term food supply would also be necessary in the event of a large-scale disaster. These events are rare, but could happen. Anything that could shut down the production, packaging, or shipping of foods for an extended period of time would be an event for which you would want long-term food storage.

Purchasing and storing quantities of food also allows you to shop for particular products when prices are lower, for example during sales or when a product is in season. You can then pull from your storage instead of purchasing those items later when the prices are high. Beating inflation, you can eat food a year from now that was purchased at today's prices.

MID-RANGE FOOD STORAGE

Long-term food storage can be divided into two time frames, mid-range foods and long-term foods. Mid-range foods are the foods that will feed you within the first year and, for the most part, can be an extension of your short-term food supply. Because many commercially or home-canned foods have

The Value of Seasonings

It is said that variety is the spice of life. Well, spices are the variety of food storage. An assortment of seasonings and sauces can go a long way toward  making your food storage more palatable over the course of time you will be eating it. Beans and rice can become Cajun beans and rice, or Mexican refried beans and Spanish rice, or Polynesian rice with beans, all with just a few different seasonings and sauces.

a shelf-life of three years or more, they can be included in a mid-range food storage plan of up to one year.

To determine what foods you need to have in your mid-range storage, you can continue with the Menu Method or Inventory Method outlined in chapter two. Substitute longer shelf-life options for any products with short shelf lives. Potatoes, for example, can store for around three months fresh, but in order to include potatoes in your mid-range storage, you will need to substitute canned or dry potatoes for the fresh ones. Multiply the ingredients out to the number of months you are planning on storing food. If you needed 12 cans of peaches for one month, you'll want to have 144 cans for a year's supply. Because of their shorter shelf lives, these foods should regularly be rotated into your normal eating routine to keep the supply fresh.

LONG-TERM FOOD STORAGE

For long-term storage, it is best to use foods with a shelf life of ten years or more. If stored properly, many foods will keep for twenty years or longer without their nutritional value deteriorating. These foods can be rotated into your normal meals or purchased and stored as insurance to be stashed in the dark corners of your basement until their shelf life is reached.

Ideal Foods for Long-term Storage

Dry foods with a moisture content of 10 percent or less are ideal for long-term storage. This includes many whole grains, dehydrated or freeze-dried foods, and powdered eggs and milk. Foods that are processed less tend to store longer. Whole wheat stores for thirty years or more, but grind that wheat into flour and the shelf life is only five years. Avoid foods with high moisture or oil content.

Shelf Life

These shelf lives apply to foods properly packaged and stored unopened in a cool, dark, dry environment.

1–3 Years
- Yeast at room temperature
- Peanut butter
- Nuts

3–5 Years
- Vegetable oil and shortening
- Drink mixes
- Hot cocoa
- Coffee
- Brown rice
- Peanut butter powder
- Home or commercially canned fruits, vegetables, and meats

5–7 Years
- Powdered eggs
- Butter powder
- Bullion
- Yeast stored in freezer
- Brown sugar
- Whole barley

10 Years
- White flour
- Sour cream powder
- Textured vegetable protein (TVP) products
- Shortening powder
- Cheese powder

20 Years
- Dehydrated fruits and vegetables
- Freeze-dried cheeses
- Powdered milk
- Dehydrated carrots
- Quinoa, rye

25 Years
- Freeze-dried fruits, vegetables, and meats
- Instant beans

30 Years
- Dry beans
- Lentils
- Rolled or whole oats
- Pearled barley
- Pasta
- Potato flakes
- Cocoa powder
- White rice
- Corn
- Wheat

Indefinite
- Sugar
- Honey
- Salt
- Baking soda
- Baking powder
- Cornstarch

THE "MORMON FOUR"

If you get down to the very basics of long-term food storage, you have what is sometimes referred to as the "Mormon Four"—wheat, beans, honey, and powdered milk. These four main food items were traditionally stored by some members of the Church of Jesus Christ of Latter-day Saints in their long-term food storage. The basis of many meals, together these four foods contain all the nutrition a body needs for survival.

1. Wheat

Wheat has been called the staff of life, and for good reason! The primary ingredient in most breads and cereals, wheat provides the body with carbohydrates,

Gluten Wheat Meat

Here are two methods for separating gluten from starch to make wheat meat.

Wheat Flour Method

1. Stir together 12 cups of whole wheat flour and 7 cups of water to create a bread-like dough. Allow the mixture to sit for twenty minutes or longer.
2. Add a small amount of water to the bowl of rested dough and squeeze the dough until the water turns milky.
3. Drain the water.
4. Place the dough in a colander and run lukewarm water over it as you continue to work the dough.
5. When the water runs off clear and the dough holds together (usually takes three to five minutes of rinsing), you have raw gluten. It may become stringy before it starts holding together, so don't give up too early!

Gluten Flour Method

You can purchase gluten flour and the process gets easier.

1. Mix 2 cups of gluten flour and ⅓ cup of whole wheat flour together
2. Add 2¼ cups of water
3. Stir together about ten stirs and you have raw gluten.

Raw gluten can be shaped as desired, then steamed or boiled. Boil in a flavored broth to add flavor the gluten. Once cooked, the gluten can be ground or sliced and eaten like meat.

protein, fiber, and a whole host of vitamins and minerals including magnesium, niacin, and zinc. Incredibly versatile, wheat can be used in a variety of ways.

Grind it: Grinding wheat will produce whole wheat flour, which you can use to make bread, flatbread, cookies, crackers, cakes, piecrusts, and more.

Separate out the gluten: Gluten is a protein-rich meat substitute. It's often called "wheat meat." After you grind wheat, you can separate the gluten from the starch using one of the methods described in the Gluten Wheat Meat sidebar.

Eat it whole: Yes, there are uses for wheat even if you don't have a grinder! You can boil the grains until soft and use them as a meat extender, make hot cereal, or eat as a side dish similar to rice. You can even chew the dry grains, although it's a little hard on the teeth.

Sprout it: Sprouting wheat boosts the vitamin content and changes the flavor. Wheat that has just started sprouting can be eaten alone or added to other foods such as salads, baked into bread, or re-dried and ground into flour. If you let the wheat sprout longer, it will grow into wheatgrass, which can be juiced or chewed straight. Wheatgrass provides protein, vitamin E, phosphorus, and potassium.

2. Beans

Dry beans come in many different varieties: white, black, pink, pinto, kidney, and lima are just a few. The "poor man's meat," beans pack a nutritional punch with fiber and protein as well as vitamin B6, iron, vitamin C, riboflavin, copper, and manganese. Beans can be used in a variety of ways.

Cook them: Soaked and boiled, beans make flavorful and filling soups. Cooked beans can also be mashed into a paste and substituted for butter in baking recipes. Mashed beans also make great refried beans.

Sprout them: You can grow them long for bean sprouts or eat them when the sprout tail is just beginning to show. At either stage they are excellent both cooked in a meal or eaten raw.

Grind them for bean flour: Grind dry beans through a grain grinder and you have bean flour. This is a great use for the older beans that don't want to soften when they are cooked. Bean flour can be used to thicken soups and stews, make instant refried beans, and can be substituted for up to one-fourth of the amount of wheat flour called for in any baking recipe's wheat flour. Beans in your cookies? You bet.

3. Honey

One of the oldest known sweeteners, honey also has an indefinite shelf life and provides carbohydrates and calories. For the best quality honey, purchase raw honey from a local beekeeper. Commercial honey may be ultra filtered or heat-processed prior to packaging, reducing the natural enzymes that provide the health benefits.

Honey can be used in a variety of ways.

Sweeten: Substitute honey for sugar in your recipes and drinks.

Heal: With honey's antibacterial properties, it can be used as a topical antibiotic for wounds and burns. Since heat kills some of the natural enzymes in honey, you will need raw honey that has not been heat-processed for best results.

Soothe: Honey works wonders to soothe sore throats as well as chapped or rough skin.

4. Powdered Milk

Milk provides protein, carbohydrates, calcium, and potassium. Powdered milk is available in instant and non-instant (also called regular) powders. The

Bean-Soaking Basics

Dry beans need to be soaked before cooking, and there are a couple of easy ways to get the soaking done.

Overnight Soak
1. Rinse beans.
2. Place in a bowl with three times as much water as beans.
3. Soak for eight hours or overnight.
4. Drain water before cooking beans.

Quick Soak
1. Rinse beans.
2. Place beans in a pot with three times as much water as beans.
3. Bring the pot to a boil and boil for two minutes.
4. Turn off heat, cover the pot, and let stand for one hour.
5. Drain water before cooking beans.

Honey Onion Cough Syrup

Ingredients:

Onion

Raw honey

Garlic, minced (optional)

Ginger root, grated (optional)

Instructions:

1. Cut your onion in thin slices across so it makes rings.
2. Put all the slices in a pot or bowl and cover with honey.
3. If desired, add minced garlic and fresh-grated ginger. Garlic has antibacterial properties, and the ginger is for flavor.
4. Allow the mixture to sit for eight to twelve hours or overnight.

After several hours, the honey and onion juice will have mixed to form a syrup. Stir it around a little bit to even out the consistency of the syrup. Then strain out the onions or just scoop the syrup you want out of the side of the pot.

Children take 1-2 teaspoons, adults 2-4 teaspoons as needed. Store in the refrigerator for up to one month.

non-instant powders are more difficult to mix into a liquid, but are also less expensive, and most mix at a lower powder-to-water ratio than their instant counterparts.

There is a lot of variation in flavor between the various brands, so do a taste test across the brands before you select one to buy for storage. Any brand you don't enjoy drinking can be used for cooking instead.

Also be aware that some powdered milks are not 100 percent milk, but rather a "milk alternative." These generally taste better for drinking, but have many other ingredients in them besides dried milk. They also will not react in the same way regular milk does when making yogurt or cheeses. If you are shopping for powdered milk, be sure to check the label—real milk will have only milk and possibly added vitamins A and D as its ingredients.

Powdered milk can be used in a variety of ways.

Drink it: Powdered milk reconstitutes into liquid milk that is ready to drink.

Use Powdered Milk to Replace Canned Milk Products

These substitutions can be used in any recipe calling for either of these canned milk products.

Evaporated Milk

    1 cup water
    ⅔ cup powdered milk

Blend together. Makes the equivalent of one 12-oz. can of evaporated milk.

Sweetened Condensed Milk

    ½ cup hot water
    1 cup sugar
    1 cup powdered milk
    3 tbsp. melted butter

Blend together until the sugar has dissolved. Makes the equivalent of one 10-oz. can of sweetened condensed milk.

Make milk-based products: Powdered milk can be made into almost any dairy product that regular milk can, including yogurt, cheeses, and even canned milk products like sweetened condensed milk or evaporated milk.

Nutrient supplement: Add dry powdered milk to recipes for some extra nutrition. It can be mixed with the dry ingredients in a baking recipe or into other foods like meat loaf or soups.

HOW MUCH FOOD DO I NEED?

Long-term food storage needs can be calculated by continuing the Menu Method or Inventory Method from chapter two; however, everything that is canned, bottled, frozen, or fresh will need replaced by a long-term storage option. This can get a little tricky but, for the most part, is possible. For example, your favorite canned enchilada sauce may now need to be stored as three different dry ingredients that you will mix into sauce when you need to use it.

You may find it easier to be a little less specific and just store quantities of foods that can be used in a variety of ways. You can use a chart like the One Year of Food Chart in this chapter (find a blank chart in the appendix) to calculate food amounts for your long-term storage. Online food storage calculators such as **lds.about.com/library/bl/faq/blcalculator.htm** can provide a good list as well.

When using a list like this to plan your family's food storage, keep in mind that these lists are frequently calculated to supply an individual with enough nutrition and calories to sustain life, not necessarily make it pleasant, so the meals may not be as filling or as flavorful as you would like. Add to it some foods your family enjoys as well as a variety of seasonings, and definitely take full advantage of the flavor and texture variations within each food group. With the wide array of options currently available for long-term food storage, there is no reason to store all 300 pounds (136kg) of grains as wheat or all 75 pounds (34kg) of dairy as powdered milk.

The quantities listed also may not be accurate for your family. You may want to add more yeast, vinegar, sugar, salt, or other items to your personal

One Year of Food Chart

The following is the suggested food storage amount for one person for one year.

- Grains (rice, pasta, flour, cereal, wheat, oats): 300 pounds (136kg)
- Legumes (beans, lentils): 60 pounds (27kg)
- Fats and oils (cooking oil, shortening): 25 pounds (11kg)
- Dairy (powdered milk, evaporated milk, cheeses): 75 pounds (34kg)
- Sugars (sugar, brown and powdered sugar, honey, drink mixes, jams and jellies): 60 pounds (27kg)
- Fruits (canned, dried, juices): 185 pounds (84kg)
- Vegetables (canned, dried): 185 pounds (84kg)
- Cooking essentials:
    Baking powder: 1 pound (454g)
    Baking soda: 1 pound (454g)
    Vinegar: ½ gallon (2L)
    Yeast: ½ pound (227g)
    Salt: 5 pounds (2kg)

Adapted from the Church of Jesus Christ of Latter-day Saints' *Essentials of Home Production and Storage* book.

storage. Increasing the quantities in each category will also help ensure that you have enough food stored. These lists also do not take into consideration any dietary restrictions you may have. A list like this is a good place to start on a long-term food storage plan; you'll just want to do a little customizing to suit the eating habits of your family.

Many food storage calculators have different calculated storage amounts for small children and adults. Children do not require as many calories as adults, but remember, this is long-term food storage, and children don't stay small forever. Some teenage children eat more than adults! To ensure you have enough food stored, I recommend calculating every member of the family as an adult.

BEYOND THE BASICS

I always advocate storing a variety of foods in your food storage, whether it be for short- or long-term. Nobody wants to eat the same foods over and over, and with the many options that are available, long-term storage can be so much more than wheat, beans, powdered milk, and honey. Dehydrated and freeze-dried fruits, vegetables, and even meats can have a shelf life of twenty-five years, which means you can still have asparagus, bell peppers, blueberries, and turkey in your long-term food storage. We'll cover more on storage options and techniques in the coming chapters. Your long-term food storage is for your family and can and should be customized to fit the needs and tastes of the individuals it will feed.

4. STORING WATER

It is easy to take water for granted. We turn on the tap, and it comes pouring out, fresh and clean and ready to use in any way we need. But what if it didn't come out? Or what if your water source was contaminated? Either of those scenarios could happen as a result of a major disaster or breakdown in the water treatment or delivery system.

In a disaster, before you need any food, you will need clean water. Contaminated water can carry a whole host of different bacteria (*E. coli*, *Giardia*) protozoa, and parasites and cause diseases including cholera. Drinking contaminated water can lead to serious illness and even death.

In most cases, it is impractical, if not impossible, to store a large amount of water. Because of this, FEMA recommends storing one gallon (4L) per person per day for two weeks. That is 14 gallons (53L) of water for each member of your family. In theory, this amount will be adequate for drinking and sanitation, however, most of us can easily use more than one gallon (4L) per day.

Try turning off your water for the day and you'll quickly realize just how many ways you use water. Calculate the water you use in a day and you'll find how fast washing, drinking, cooking, and more add up. The easiest solution to having clean water in an emergency is to have some stored in one of the various available water storage containers.

WATER STORAGE OPTIONS
Store-Bought Gallons of Water
You can purchase jugs of drinking water that look like milk jugs, commonly found in most grocery and variety stores.

Ways to Conserve Water

Your water supply will go much farther if you conserve water during an emergency. Here are some quick ideas to save on water usage:

- Use hand sanitizer instead of washing hands.
- Use disinfecting wipes to clean food-prep and eating areas.
- Use body cleaning wipes instead of showering.
- Try a dry shampoo to de-grease your hair.

Pros

- inexpensive, usually less than a dollar per gallon
- readily available at most stores
- manageable weight

Cons

- thin jug plastic has a short shelf life and frequently develops leaks
- cannot be stacked

Water Bottles

The single-serving kind can be purchased individually or by the case.

Pros

- readily available at many stores
- inexpensive if purchased by the case
- portable, single serve, and resealable
- cases can be stacked

Cons

- small, so you need many to get your 1-gallon-per-person-per-day quota, especially for a large family
- make a lot of waste

Reused PETE Bottles

Two-liter soda bottles are inexpensive examples of PETE (polyethylene terephthalate) bottles. Empty soda bottles offer an almost free water storage option that you would otherwise be throwing away. Offer to help clean up after a party and you can go home with a bunch of them! Wash them with dish soap and sanitize by rinsing with a mixture of ten parts water to one part bleach (e.g., 10 cups water to 1 cup bleach) before filling.

Twelve Emergency Water Uses

For the first six needs, clean, purified water is best.

1. Drinking. Obviously water is essential for your survival. Staying properly hydrated keeps your mind sharp and your energy level up.
2. Personal hygiene. Keeping yourself clean will discourage the spread of disease, plus it's a huge morale booster.
3. Washing food. Keeping food clean will keep everyone healthier.
4. Cooking. Most "from scratch" meals use some kind of liquid, usually water.
5. Rehydrating all your dry food storage. Dehydrated, freeze-dried, or powdered foods including infant formula will need water to reconstitute them.
6. Wound care. Even little scrapes can turn into a big deal if they're left dirty or cleaned with contaminated water.
7. Flushing toilets. Pour water into the tank and flush with the lever like usual, or pour the water directly into the bowl (slowly) and gravity takes over and all the goods go down the pipes.
8. Washing clothes. Not too high on the imperative list, but a very nice morale boost.
9. Watering animals. If you're planning on keeping livestock, chickens, pets, etc. alive, they'll need water to drink.
10. Watering a garden. Supplemental watering can mean the difference between harvesting a garden or just putting seeds in dirt.
11. Keeping food cool. A Zeer pot is a device that keeps food cool through evaporation. It consists of two nested pots with wet sand packed between them. The action of the water evaporating from the sand cools the food stored inside the inner pot.
12. Keeping people cool. Use the water to dampen clothing, hats, or neckerchiefs, or apply directly on the skin to keep cool on a hot day. Evaporative cooling techniques work best in a low-humidity environment.

Pros

- practically free
- good size to fit in little unused spaces in your house like behind the couch or in a closet
- easy to carry—they weigh only about 4½ pounds (2kg) when full

Cons

- difficult to stack
- need to be thoroughly cleaned before filling with water
- water should be rotated every six to twelve months, more frequently than commercially filled bottles

Water Bricks

Waterbricks

Waterbricks are plastic, cube-shaped containers that hold 3½ gallons (13L) of water and can stack like building blocks.

Pros

- weigh only 28 pounds (13kg) full and come with carrying handles
- wide mouth opening makes for easy cleaning
- stable when stacked
- low profile—can fit under a bed
- available spout makes dispensing water easy

Cons

- expensive—cost about seventeen dollars each, plus more for the spout

Five-Gallon Hard Plastic Jugs

Five-gallon jugs come in a variety of shapes and colors and can be found in most stores that sell camping equipment, as well as in many emergency supply retailers.

Pros

- sturdy construction
- available spout attachments dispense water easily
- hold approximately one day's worth of water for a family of four or five

Cons

- slightly more expensive than other options
- moderately heavy, about 40 pounds (18kg) each when full
- some are designed to stack, but others aren't, so they can use up a lot of floor space

Water Stored Around the Home

Don't forget that there are places in your home where you already have clean water that you could use in an emergency:

- water heater
- pipes
- ice cube trays

Water that isn't safe to drink but could be used for other purposes during an emergency:

- toilet tank
- water bed
- swimming pool

Bathtub Water Bladder

In an emergency situation, you can fill your bathtub with water to create a reserve of water. Before you fill the tub, fit it with a bathtub water bladder such as the AquaPod to keep the water clean and contained.

Pros
- holds as much water as your bathtub
- packs small when not in use

Cons
- most are designed for one-time use
- designed to be filled right before an emergency
- sharp-clawed indoor pets can damage the bladder
- tub is unavailable for anything else when the water bladder is in use

30- to 55-Gallon Drum

Large plastic barrels that can hold 30 to 55 gallons (114 to 208L) of water are available at most emergency supply retailers.

Pros
- large volume
- small footprint for the amount of water they hold

Cons
- cost
- very heavy, so very difficult to move when full

- need a pump or siphon system to get water out
- bulky—it might be tough to find a place for one of these in a small home
- round shape can leave wasted space in corners where it is stored

Water Storage Tank
A few manufacturers have created water storage tanks that can hold between 160 and 320 gallons (606L and 1,121L).

Pros
- very large volume
- some are rectangular-shaped, so there is no wasted corner space
- easy to dispense water when using the attached spouts
- most have vents that let air in, allowing water to flow out smoothly

Cons
- cost
- weight
- require a large space for storage—again maybe not a good fit for a small home

FILLING YOUR CONTAINERS
If you are filling a clean container with water from a municipal source that has been treated with chlorine, no additional water treatment is necessary. If your water comes from a well or other source that has not been treated, add two drops of unscented regular bleach to each gallon of water before storing.

Fill your containers to the top unless they will be stored where they might freeze. A container subjected to freezing temperatures should be filled only 85 percent full to allow room for the water to expand without breaking the container, and should be constructed of plastic that can withstand freezing temperatures.

Put the lid on your containers tightly and write the date on each one so you know when it was filled. This date will help you know when it's time for rotation.

STORAGE
Keep your water containers in a ventilated, cool, dark, dry place whenever possible. Use boards or pallets to keep them off the ground. Elevating the containers keeps them dry underneath and also keeps the plastic from absorbing any chemicals from the floor it is sitting on. Water containers made of

polyethylene plastic with recycle code 2 can absorb fumes, so storing these containers in a garage with vehicle exhaust can change the flavor of the water over time and even make it unfit to drink.

ROTATION

After all your storage containers are filled with water, it's time to think about rotating that water. FEMA recommends that stored water be rotated every six to twelve months. Water does not have an expiration date, so if it is not rotated, it likely will still be safe to drink even years later. However, because most large water containers will be filled on site and not in a sterile factory, there is the possibility of having some type of contaminant in the water. Frequent rotation will reset the clock on any contaminants in your water storage. Rotating your water supply also keeps it tasting as fresh as possible.

Water you are rotating out can be used to water your garden, lawn, or animals. Rinse and refill your containers. Don't forget to write the new date on the container when you're finished. One way to remember when to rotate your water is to note it on your long-term food storage inventory list. Another trick is to rotate the water on holidays such as New Year's Day and Independence Day.

NATURAL SOURCES

Water for emergency use can be found and secured from natural sources. Lakes, rivers, and streams hold large amounts of emergency water. This water won't be clean, so use it for a purpose that does not require clean water or have a method to make the water safe to drink. Avoid water that is dark colored, has floating matter, or has a bad odor. Check upstream from your water source for anything that might be a contaminant, and do not use water that has human or animal waste in it. Flood water should also be avoided.

You may not live right next to a natural water source, but there are probably some near enough that you could walk to them. Map out your local fresh water resources—lakes, reservoirs, rivers, streams, and springs. Plan on a way to transport the water you need from the source to your location. Water weighs 8 pounds (4kg) per gallon (4L), so it can get heavy very quickly. Use containers that you can lift when full, and think about wheeled options you could use to make moving the water easier. Carts, wagons, strollers, and bike trailers are all good options when a vehicle can't be used.

RAIN BARRELS

Using rain barrels to catch free water from the sky is an easy and inexpensive way to add to your water storage. You can build a rain barrel system with very

The parts of a rain barrel:

1. Downspout: Funnels the collected rain into the barrel.
2. Screen: Keeps large debris out of the collected water.
3. Overflow pipe: Diverts excess water away from the home's foundation or into an additional barrel.
4. Spigot: Near the bottom of the barrel for easy access to the collected water.
5. Base: Place the barrel on a solid base of gravel or cement. Raising the barrel on cinder blocks increases the output water pressure.

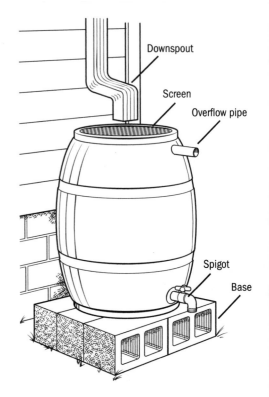

little investment or purchase a premade system. Either type works on the same concept. Rain falling on a roof is diverted through a debris-catching screen and into a container, usually through the gutter system that is already on the house. The water that would normally run down the spout and into the ground or down the sidewalk now is contained in a barrel and can be used when needed to water plants or animals, or purified for drinking, washing, and cooking. Barrels can be linked together to provide a higher volume of stored water. A spigot near the bottom of the barrel makes the water easy to access.

Unfortunately, some states have regulations regarding the use of rain barrels, and in a few states it is illegal to collect rain water, so be sure to check your local regulations before installing a rain barrel system.

WELLS

If you have access to a well, you've got a whole lot of water available to you. Wells do have a few drawbacks, so if you are planning on using a well for your emergency water source, consider these:

- Most wells have electric pumps, so if the power is off, you won't have access to that water unless you have a manual pump available or can connect the electric pump to a generator.

- Wells can be disturbed during natural disasters like earthquakes, so don't make a well your only source of stored water.
- Sometimes wells do not produce drinking-quality water to begin with, so it's best to drink water from wells only if they have been tested safe prior to the disaster, or be prepared to treat any well water you intend to consume.

PURIFICATION OPTIONS

Being able to purify water to drink is very important. It is unlikely you will be able to store the full amount of water your family will need in an emergency situation, so having a way to purify other water sources will fill the gaps and allow you to drink clean water as long as you need to. Purified water can be obtained by a variety of methods.

Heat

Water pasteurization is accomplished by heating water to 149°F (65°C) for a few minutes. Boiling water brings it to 212°F (100°C). Although it is not necessary to boil water to render it safe to drink, boiling is an excellent visual indicator that the water has reached temperatures high enough to free it from microbes, including *E. coli, Rotavirus, Giardia,* and the hepatitis A virus. Pasteurization does not remove sediment from water, so if your water source has a lot of sediment in it, prefilter the water through a cloth prior to pasteurization, or allow it to settle and skim the clear water off the top.

Water can be heated for pasteurization on a stove or by using solar power. To use the sun, a solar oven is ideal, but other methods can get your water hot enough to pasteurize it as well. Try the dash of your vehicle, a metal roof, or just a black container in the sun on a hot day.

SODIS

Solar water disinfection (SODIS) uses a combination of the sun's UV-A rays and heat from the infrared rays to pasteurize water. SODIS is primarily used in developing countries to provide simple and inexpensive safe water. Because the sun's rays are not equally strong at every location on the earth, SODIS works best between the latitudes of 15° and 35° north of the equator and 15° and 35° south of the equator. The area between 15° north and 15° south also gets enough direct sun to use SODIS. These parameters include some of the southern part of the United States.

To disinfect water with the SODIS method:

1. Use clear water. Water with high turbidity does not purify well, so pre-filter the water through a cloth to remove large debris, let sediment settle to the bottom of a container, and skim off the clear water for purifying.
2. Fill a clean PETE bottle three-quarters full of water. For best results, the bottle should be no more than 4 inches (10cm) across.
3. Shake to aerate (higher oxygen levels aid in the disinfection rate).
4. Fill the rest of the bottle with water.
5. Lay the bottle in direct sunlight for six hours. It works even better if the bottle is laid on a light-reflecting surface like a metal roof, or even a Mylar blanket. After six hours it is safe to drink.

Distillation

Distillation is the process of collecting and condensing water vapor. When water vaporizes, either through boiling or evaporation, that vapor leaves behind any impurities. The distilled water is then purified and clean to drink. Distillation rids water of particulate matter, minerals, viruses and bacteria, radiation fallout, and even salt. By distilling water, you can create drinkable water from any contaminated water.

The easiest way to distill water at home is through boiling.

1. Fill a large pot with water.
2. Place a bowl in the pot so it floats. A bowl that is just slightly smaller in diameter than the pot works best. If it does not float, set a rack in the pot so the bowl doesn't sit on the bottom of the pot.
3. Bring the water to a boil.
4. Place the lid of the pot on so it slopes inward. Most pot lids will be used upside down.
5. Add ice to the outside of the lid to speed the condensing process.
6. All the water that falls from the lid into the bowl is distilled and free from any harmful bacteria, viruses, or sediment.

CHEMICAL PURIFICATION TREATMENTS

Another simple method for purifying water is chemical treatment, which primarily comes in two forms: iodine and chlorine. Any of the chemical treatments can leave a bad taste in your water. Flavor can be improved by adding powdered drink mixes such as Gatorade. To get rid of a chlorine taste, you can encourage dissipation of the chlorine by transferring the water back and forth between two containers.

What in the World Is a WAPI?

Water is pasteurized at 149°F (65°C), well below the boiling point. So if your water does not reach boiling temperatures, how can you know it got hot enough to be safe to drink? Use a WAPI (pronounced WAH-pee), which is short for Water Pasteurization Indicator. It is a simple, inexpensive temperature indicator that consists of a clear, plastic tube about 1¾" (5cm) long that

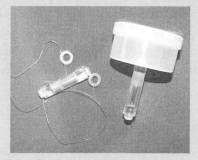

Wire and floating Water Pasteurization Indicators (WAPI)

contains a small amount of heat-sensitive soy wax at one end of the tube. The tube is weighted or suspended from a float so it remains vertical in the water. Place the WAPI in the water with the wax at the top of the tube. The wax melts at 150°F (66°C) and will completely fall to the bottom of the tube after six minutes at that temperature (long enough to fully pasteurize the water). The melted wax will stay at the bottom of the tube, so you'll know your water reached pasteurization temperatures even if it cools before you check it. After the wax cools, you can turn the tube over again so the wax is back at the top and use the WAPI over and over again.

Iodine

Iodine treatment is commonly found in tablets that can be purchased at most outdoor or camping stores. These tablets have been used by the military for over fifty years. Each tablet releases 8 milligrams of iodine into the water, which penetrates the cell walls of the microorganisms, rendering them inactive and making the water safe to drink. Use two tablets per quart or liter of water and wait twenty to thirty minutes for full protection. An unopened bottle has a shelf life of at least four years. Always follow the directions on the package.

Liquid iodine tincture can also be added to water at a rate of five drops per quart or liter of water. Stir the iodine throughout the water and wait thirty minutes before drinking. Use double the amount for cloudy water. Iodine is a short-term water purification solution and shouldn't be used for more than three consecutive months due to the possibility of liver damage.

Chlorine

Chlorine is another chemical water purification option. The simplest way to treat your water with chlorine is to use regular bleach (sodium hypochlorite). Sodium hypochlorite in the concentration of 5.25 percent to 6 percent should be the only active ingredient in the bleach. There should not be any added soap or fragrances. A major bleach manufacturer has also added sodium hydroxide as an active ingredient, which they state does not pose a health risk for water treatment.

Add sixteen drops of liquid chlorine bleach per gallon (4L) of water, or four drops per quart or liter of water. Stir to mix, and let stand thirty minutes. If it smells of chlorine, it is ready to use. If it does not smell of chlorine, repeat the process, including the wait time, and smell it again. If, after two attempts, it does not smell of chlorine, discard it and find another source of water.

Bleach will lose its potency over time, so it is best to use bleach that is less than six months old.

Chlorine Powder

Another way to treat water with chlorine is to use calcium hypochlorite, which is a dry, granular chlorine that is sold for swimming pool use, the most common brand being Pool Shock. Granular calcium hypochlorite has the advantage of a much longer shelf life than liquid bleach. Purifying water with calcium hypochlorite is a two-step process:

1. Add and dissolve one heaping teaspoon of high-test granular calcium hypochlorite (approximately ¼ ounce) for each 2 gallons of water, or use 5 milliliters (approximately 7 grams) per 7½ liters of water. This mixture produces a chlorine solution. Do not drink this solution.

2. To disinfect water, add the chlorine solution in the ratio of one part of chlorine solution to each one hundred parts of water to be treated, approximately 2 teaspoons (10mL) per quart or liter. Let the treated water sit for at least three minutes before using.

Chlorine Dioxide

Chlorine dioxide tablets are a third chemical treatment option. Chlorine dioxide is different from chlorine bleach and works through oxidation rather than chlorination. These tablets leave water tasting better than iodine tablets or liquid chlorine and are manufactured by Aquamira, Katadyn, and Potable Aqua. Chlorine dioxide tablets' average shelf life is five years, and they are sized to use one tablet per quart or liter (always read the instructions on any water purification tablets you purchase).

Chemical Treatment Chart

METHOD	AMOUNT TO TREAT 1 QUART/ LITER	AMOUNT TO TREAT 1 GALLON (4L)	WAIT TIME
Iodine tablets	2 tablets	8 tablets	20–30 minutes
Iodine tincture	5-10 drops	20 drops	30 minutes
Liquid bleach	4 drops	16 drops	30 minutes
Granular chlorine	2 tsp. (10mL) of mixed solution	8 tsp. (3mL) of mixed solution	30 minutes
Chlorine dioxide tablets	1 tablet	4 tablets	4 hours

PURIFICATION BY WATER FILTERS

There are a wide variety of filtration systems available that would produce enough water for extended use, and they all work in generally the same way. Water molecules are smaller than waterborne pathogens, so filters work like dumping pasta in a colander, only on a much smaller scale. The water flows through the filter, and the pathogens get caught. The size of pores on the filter determines which pathogens are allowed through. Most filters will catch protozoa and bacteria. A few, usually labeled as water purifiers instead of filters, also catch or neutralize viruses. Some catch viruses by having a very small pore size, and some have a chemical additive in the system that will neutralize viruses.

When looking for a family-sized water filtration system, here's what you'll want to look for.

Pump or Gravity

This is a personal preference. A gravity-fed filter uses gravity to force the water through the filter. With a pump filter, water must be manually pumped to get the water through. Usually a pump filter will produce clean water at a faster rate than a gravity-fed filter; however, it also takes more work. Gravity-fed filters can filter water while you are doing something else and are generally less expensive than their group-sized pump counterparts.

Flow Rate

You want a filter that will provide clean water at a rate that provides for the needs of your family. Also check how that flow rate is accomplished. Some filters increase flow rate by increasing pore size, others use more than one filter within the unit, and others have an increased filter surface area.

Filter Gallon Capacity

This number tells you how many gallons the unit can filter before needing to be replaced. If this number is not as high as you would like, there is usually an option to purchase replacement filters without purchasing a second filtration unit.

Design

This will vary greatly between pump and gravity-fed styles, but even within the gravity-fed category there are a few variations. Some filters are a freestanding unit, like the Berkey filtration systems. Others, like the Sawyer Point Zero Two and the AquaPail, either attach to a bucket or are integrated into one and need a container to dispense the clean water into.

SUMMARY

Whether you plan to store all your water, purify it as needed, or do some of both, get some water storage started. It could save you from some minor inconveniences, or it could save your life.

5. PRESERVING YOUR OWN FOOD

Preserving your own fresh food can provide your family with a large variety of food storage for very little cost. Produce, whether grown in your garden or purchased at stores or farmers markets, and hunted or purchased meats don't stay fresh forever. Make the best use of an abundance of fresh foods by canning, dehydrating, or freezing them for later use.

CANNING

Home canning of foods was developed in the late 1700s as a method for providing food for Napoleon's armies. In the 1930s and '40s, increased safety measures and availability of home-canning products combined with an economic downturn and war-induced food rations caused a dramatic increase in the popularity of home canning. While canning is not as prevalent as it once was, it is still a fantastic way to preserve your own foods. As a general rule, home-canned foods have an optimal shelf life of one year and are best used before two years.

Benefits of Home Canning

Home canning has many benefits. It allows you to preserve excess food so it is not wasted if you can't eat it all before it goes bad. Once foods are canned, it is very convenient to have a pantry stocked with foods that are cooked and ready to eat when the jar is opened. Home canning also gives you complete control over the quality and type of foods you eat from a can. Customize what you seal in your jars to suit your tastes or food restrictions.

Supplies

For proper home canning, you'll need a few basic supplies. While there are many tools that are nice to have, these are the ones you'll really need to get started.

Water bath canner: If you are new to canning, most people start with a water bath canner. A water bath canner consists of a large pot with a lid and a slotted or wire rack that fits inside the pot to hold the jars off the bottom of the pot. The pot needs to be deep enough that there is at least 1 inch (3cm) of rapidly boiling water over the tops of the jars when they are processing. Commercially produced water bath canners come in aluminum, stainless steel, and porcelain-covered steel that is usually blue or black with white specks (called granite ware). These canners are inexpensive (generally between twenty and ninety dollars) and can sometimes even be found at yard sales and thrift stores. Use a water bath canner for processing foods high in acid, like fruits, pickles, and most tomato products. To can low-acid foods, you will need a steam pressure canner in addition to your water canner.

Steam pressure canner: Steam pressure canners are available in either aluminum or stainless steel. They have a fitted lid with a steam vent and pressure gauge, and an interior rack to raise the jars off the bottom of the canner. A steam pressure

Water bath canner

Steam pressure canner

Canning supplies: Jar lifter, jar, two-piece caps, funnel

Reusable Canning Lids

While most canning lids are made for one-time use, a company called Tattler produces lids that are reusable. The lids are made in wide-mouth and narrow-mouth sizes and consist of a plastic lid and a rubber gasket. The plastic lids can be used over and over, and the gaskets (which can be purchased separate from the lids) are good for ten uses each. If you are planning on continu-

Tattler reusable canning lids

ing to can food in a long-term emergency, you'll either need to invest in a large supply of the disposable lids or stock some of these reusable lids.

canner is more expensive than a water bath canner (ranging from eighty-five to three hundred dollars) and is used to can low-acid foods like meats and non-pickled vegetables. A pressure cooker is similar to a pressure canner, but does not include the weighted or dial gauge, so cannot be safely used for canning.

Jar: Mason jars by brands like Kerr, Ball, and Golden Harvest are made to withstand the heat and pressure associated with repeated uses of home canning. They are available in sizes ranging from half pint to half gallon, with pint and quart size being the most common. Each jar volume also has the option of either a wide-mouth or a narrow- (commonly called regular) mouth opening. Canning jars can also occasionally be found at yard sales or thrift stores. If purchasing them used, check each jar and its opening thoroughly for chips or cracks before buying.

Two-piece caps: A cap to seal a jar comes in two pieces, the lid and the ring. Metal canning lids have a sealing material around the outside edge of the underside of the lid. They are made for single use and come in both wide- and narrow-mouth sizes. Rings screw onto the jars, securing the lid to the jar, and are also available in both mouth sizes.

Jar funnel: This specially designed funnel, available wherever canning supplies are sold, helps you get the food into the jars without leaving a mess on the counter, stove top, or jar rims.

Jar lifter: These specialized tongs are designed to lift hot jars from the canner.

Standardize Jar Openings

If you are purchasing all your jars new, it is easy to choose either wide- or narrow-mouth jars and buy them all the same. This will simplify your canning lid purchases, and you'll always know how many of which lids you'll need to complete your canning project.

However, you may find that it is worth storing and sorting both lid sizes if you end up with a mix of jar mouth sizes by obtaining jars inexpensively from a thrift store, yard sale, or giveaway.

Canning Safety

Ensure the quality and safety of your home-canned goods by using proper canning procedures.

- Start with high-quality produce or meats, discarding any that are bruised or spoiled. Process foods shortly after obtaining them while they are still fresh—within twenty-four hours is best.
- Be clean. Keep your work area and equipment clean, and pack food into sterilized jars.
- Get your canning recipes from a reputable source, and always use the proper canning technique, including recommended times and pressures, for the foods you are canning. Don't forget to adjust for altitude.

Using a Water Bath Canner

Canning in a water bath canner is an inexpensive and easy way to get started canning. Regardless of what product you choose to can, the process is generally the same.

Preparation: Fill your canner about half full of water and start heating it. Heat extra water or mix and heat syrup as needed for your canning project, and heat your jar lids in a small pan of water. Prepare your fruit by pitting, peeling, coring, and slicing as needed. Treat the fruit in a color-preserving acidic soak if desired (see the Preserve That Pretty Color sidebar in this chapter). Fill the jars using either the hot-pack or raw-pack method.

Canning: Once the jars are full, place the hot lids on and screw the rings on finger tight (that is, as tight as can be made using the strength of your fingers). Place the hot jars on the rack in the canner and lower the rack so the jars are covered with at least 1 inch (3cm) of water. Put the lid on the canner, heat the water to a rolling boil, then start the processing time. Keep the water boiling

Canning Above Sea Level

Because water boils at a lower temperature at higher altitudes, for foods to be safe from spoilage, adjustments need to be made to either processing time or pressure when canning at altitudes higher than 1,000 feet (305m) above sea level.

WATER BATH CANNER	
ALTITUDE (FEET)	INCREASE PROCESSING TIME
1,001-3,000	5 minutes
3,001-6,000	10 minutes
6,001-8,000	15 minutes
8,001-10,000	20 minutes

STEAM PRESSURE CANNER		
ALTITUDE (FEET)	WEIGHTED GAUGE	DIAL GAUGE
0-1,000	10	11
1,001-2,000	15	11
2,001-4,000	15	12
4,001-6,000	15	13
6,001-8,000	15	14
8,001-10,000	15	15

during the entire processing time. When the jars are done processing, turn off the heat. Remove the jars from the canner and place them on a rack to cool. Check the seals once the jars are completely cool. Label each jar with the food name and canning date before putting them in your cupboard.

WATER BATH CANNING INSTRUCTIONS
Apples
To prepare, wash, core, and peel the apples. Slice, quarter, or halve. Pretreat for color retention; drain.

- **To raw pack:** Raw pack is not recommended.
- **To hot pack:** Boil in syrup five minutes. Pack hot fruit and syrup in hot jars, leaving ½ inch (1cm) headspace. Process pints and quarts twenty minutes.

Applesauce

To prepare, wash, stem, and quarter the apples. Cook until soft in a pot with a small amount of water. Press apples through a food sieve to separate pulp from seeds and peels. Add sugar to taste, and simmer until desired thickness.

- **To raw pack:** Cannot raw pack.
- **To hot pack:** Pour hot applesauce in hot jars, leaving ½ inch (1cm) headspace. Process pints and quarts twenty minutes.

Apricots

To prepare, wash, halve, and remove pits.

- **To raw pack:** Fill jars and add boiling syrup, leaving ½ inch (1cm) headspace. Process pints twenty minutes, quarts twenty-five minutes.
- **To hot pack:** Add fruit to hot syrup and bring to a boil. Pack hot fruit and syrup in jars, leaving ½ inch (1cm) headspace. Process pints twenty minutes, quarts twenty-five minutes.

Preserve That Pretty Color

Many fruits develop an off color or turn brown quickly after being cut or canned. Pretty peaches and pears are a lot more appetizing than brown ones, and preserving the color is easy with an acidic soak.

To 1 quart (1L) of cold water, add any one of the following:
- Commercially packaged color preserver like Fruit-Fresh or EverFresh according to label instructions
- 2½ tablespoons ascorbic acid powder
- three 500 mg vitamin C tablets, crushed
- 1 teaspoon citric acid powder
- ½ cup (118mL) lemon juice

Stir to dissolve. Dip the fruit into the mixture as soon after cutting as possible to prevent browning. Soak fruit in the solution for five to ten minutes, then remove fruit and proceed with canning.

Syrups for Fruit

When canning fruit, you'll need to add syrup to the jars. Use a lighter syrup for very sweet fruit, and heavier syrup for tart fruit. Syrups can also be used when freezing fruits.

- For a light syrup use: 2 cups sugar, 4 cups water
- For a medium syrup use: 3 cups sugar, 4 cups water
- For a heavy syrup use: 4½ cups sugar, 4 cups water

Heat the sugar and water in a pot until the sugar dissolves. Continue adding sugar and water as needed to finish the canning job. Use syrup hot for canning or let it cool to use for freezing.

Berries

To prepare, wash berries in cold water.

- **To raw pack:** Raw packing is best for berries like raspberries that don't hold their shape well when heated. Ladle ½ cup of hot syrup into jar. Gently fill with berries and add more syrup as needed, leaving ½ inch (1cm) headspace. Process pints fifteen minutes, quarts twenty minutes.
- **To hot pack:** Best for berries that hold their shape when heated (like blackberries). Place washed berries in a bowl and add ½ cup sugar for each quart of berries. Stir and let stand for two hours. Heat slowly until the sugar dissolves. Ladle hot berries and syrup into jars. Process pints and quarts fifteen minutes.

Cherries

To prepare, wash and pit if desired.

- **To raw pack:** Fill jars and add boiling syrup, leaving ½ inch (1cm) headspace. Process pints fifteen minutes, quarts twenty minutes.
- **To hot pack:** Add cherries to hot syrup and bring to boiling. Fill jars with hot fruit and syrup, leaving ½ inch (1cm) headspace. Process pints fifteen minutes, quarts twenty minutes.

Peaches

To prepare, peel by submerging in boiling water two to three minutes, then into cold water and slipping off the skins. Halve or slice, removing pits. Treat to prevent discoloration.

- **To raw pack:** Fill jars and add boiling syrup, leaving ½ inch (1cm) headspace. Process pints twenty minutes, quarts twenty-five minutes.
- **To hot pack:** Add fruit to hot syrup and bring to a boil. Pack hot fruit and syrup in jars. Process pints twenty minutes, quarts twenty-five minutes.

Pears

To prepare, wash, peel, core, cut into quarters or halves, and treat to prevent browning.
- **To raw pack:** Raw packing is not recommended.
- **To hot pack:** Add fruit to hot syrup, bring to a boil, and simmer five minutes. Pack hot fruit and syrup in jars, leaving ½ inch (1cm) headspace. Process pints twenty minutes, quarts twenty-five minutes.

Tomatoes

To prepare, wash, peel by submerging in boiling water two to three minutes then into cold water and slipping off skins. Core and leave whole or cut in quarters, eighths, or dices.
- **To raw pack:** Raw packing is not recommended.
- **To hot pack:** Heat tomatoes in a pot with just enough water to prevent sticking. Bring to a boil, and simmer five minutes. Add 1 tablespoon lemon juice or ¼ teaspoon citric acid to each pint jar, 2 tablespoons lemon juice or ½ teaspoon citric acid to each quart. Fill with hot tomatoes and liquid, leaving ½ inch (1cm) headspace. Add ½ teaspoon salt to each pint, 1 teaspoon salt to each quart if desired. Process pints forty minutes, quarts forty-five minutes.

USING A STEAM PRESSURE CANNER

Don't be intimidated by pressure canners! Although they are a little more complex and expensive than a water bath canner, they are easy to use and the only safe method to can low-acid foods at home.

Preparation

Fill your canner with 2–3 inches (5–8cm) of water and start heating it on low. Some canners have a fill line engraved on the inside for reference. Heat extra water as needed for your canning project, and heat your jar lids in a small pan of water. Prepare your food by washing, peeling, and slicing as needed. Fill the jars with the food and water as directed in the canning instructions.

Gauging Pressure

If you are relying on your canner's dial gauge to identify the pressure you are canning at, you'll need to periodically get the gauge tested for accuracy. Contact your county extension office for the nearest testing location. (Find your local office at www.csrees.usda.gov/Extension.) It only takes a couple of minutes, and you just need to take the lid, not the whole canner. Older canners should be checked at least once a year.

An alternative to getting your dial gauge tested is to use a weighted gauge. These are the weights that sit on top of your canner's steam pipe. The heaviest are made to rock at 15 lbs. pressure, which is plenty of pressure to can at even high altitudes. Some weighted gauges come in pieces so you can have the weight rock at 5 lbs., 10 lbs., or 15 lbs. These weights take some of the babysitting out of canning with a pressure canner. Just adjust the heat so the weight is rocking gently and the pressure will stay even without having to watch the dial. Using a weighted gauge also allows you to keep using a lid with a dial gauge that isn't accurate.

Canning

Place the hot lids on the filled jars and screw the rings on finger tight. Place the hot jars on the rack in the bottom of the pressure canner. The jars will not be covered with water. Secure the lid on the canner following the manufacturer's instructions without placing the weight on the steam pipe. Heat the water and jars to a rolling boil. Allow the steam to vent for a few minutes before putting the weight on the steam pipe. Once the weight is on the pipe, the pressure will build inside the canner. Begin the processing time when the canner has reached the correct pressure for your altitude. Adjust the heat to keep the pressure as constant as possible throughout the processing time. When the jars are done processing, remove the canner from the heat and allow it to cool on its own. When the pressure gauge is down, remove the lid and move the jars from the canner to a cooling rack. Check the seals once the jars are completely cool. Label with the food name and canning date before putting the jars in your cupboard.

STEAM PRESSURE CANNING INSTRUCTIONS
Beans (green or wax)

To prepare, wash and remove the stems and ends. Remove the strings. Leave whole or snap into 1–2 inch (3–5cm) pieces.

To process, pack into jars. Add ½ teaspoon salt per pint, 1 teaspoon salt per quart if desired. Add boiling water, leaving 1 inch (3cm) headspace. Process pints twenty minutes, quarts twenty-five minutes at 10 lbs. pressure.

Beets
To prepare, wash, trim tops, steam until tender. Cool, peel, and slice or cube.

To process, pack into jars. Add ½ teaspoon salt per pint, 1 teaspoon salt per quart if desired. Add boiling water, leaving 1 inch (3cm) headspace. Process pints thirty minutes, quarts thirty-five minutes at 10 lbs. pressure.

Carrots
To prepare, wash and peel carrots. Slice, dice, or leave whole.

To process, pack into jars. Add ½ teaspoon salt per pint, 1 teaspoon salt per quart if desired. Add boiling water, leaving 1 inch (3cm) headspace. Process pints twenty-five minutes, quarts thirty minutes at 10 lbs. pressure.

Corn
To prepare, shuck, removing the husks and silk. Wash. Cut corn from the cob.

To process, pack loosely into jars, do not shake or press in. Add ½ teaspoon salt per pint, 1 teaspoon salt per quart as desired. Add boiling water, leaving 1 inch (3cm) headspace. Process pints fifty-five minutes, quarts eighty-five minutes at 10 lbs. pressure.

Greens (spinach, kale, chard, beet, turnip)
To prepare, wash thoroughly. Trim the tough stems. Cook in a small amount of water just until wilted. Cut larger greens into pieces.

To process, pack hot greens into hot jars. Add ½ teaspoon salt per pint, 1 teaspoon per quart as desired. Add boiling water, leaving 1 inch (3cm) headspace. Process pints seventy minutes, quarts ninety minutes at 10 lbs. pressure.

Meat (chicken, pork, beef, game meats)
To prepare, trim the fat and cut meat into strips or cubes.

To process, pack meat into jars. Add ½ teaspoon salt per pint, 1 teaspoon salt per quart as desired. Add boiling water, leaving 1 inch (3cm) headspace. Process pints seventy-five minutes, quarts ninety minutes at 10 lbs. pressure.

Mixed vegetables
To prepare, wash and prepare vegetables as for individual canning.

To process, combine the vegetables in a sauce pot, cover with water, and

Earthquake-Proof Your Canning

If you live in an earthquake zone, you'll want to take extra precautions with your canned foods. Jars placed on a shelf can easily fall off and break, ruining the food you had stored in them. Here are some ideas to help earthquake-proof your canned foods:

JarBOX plastic jar storage totes

- Repack the filled jars in their original box or another box they will fit tightly in. Years ago, jars came in full boxes that they fit in very tightly, but even the half boxes they are sold in now will slow down sliding caused by an earthquake. Canning jar boxes can also be purchased at uline.com, a packaging supply company.
- Use a JarBOX. These plastic totes are kind of pricey, but are specially designed for packing and protecting canning jars.
- Store your canned foods low in your storage area. Jars stored high have farther to fall.
- Install braces on the front of your food storage shelves. A board or barrier across the uprights will help keep the jars from sliding off the shelf.

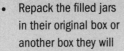

boil five minutes. Pack hot vegetables and water in hot jars, leaving 1 inch (3cm) headspace. Add ½ teaspoon salt per pint, 1 teaspoon salt per quart as desired. Process pints fifty-five minutes, quarts eighty-five minutes at 10 lbs. pressure.

Okra

To prepare, wash, drain, and remove the stem and blossom end. Leave whole or slice.

To process, boil two minutes and pack hot okra into hot jars. Add ½ teaspoon salt per pint, 1 teaspoon salt per quart. Add boiling water, leaving 1 inch (3cm) headspace. Process pints twenty-five minutes, quarts forty minutes at 10 lbs. pressure.

PRESERVING YOUR OWN FOOD

Peas (green)

To prepare, shell and wash peas.

To process, pack loosely into jars. Add ½ teaspoon salt per pint, 1 teaspoon salt per quart as desired. Add boiling water, leaving 1 inch (3cm) headspace. Process pints or quarts forty minutes at 10 lbs. pressure.

Potatoes

To prepare, peel and wash potatoes. Quarter large potatoes, leave small potatoes whole.

To process, boil ten minutes. Pack hot potatoes into hot jars. Add ½ teaspoon salt per pint, 1 teaspoon salt per quart. Add boiling water, leaving 1 inch (3cm) headspace. Process pints thirty-five minutes, quarts forty minutes at 10 lbs. pressure.

FOODS NOT SAFE FOR HOME CANNING

Although canning is an excellent method of preservation for many foods, some foods should not be home canned, either due to their inability to heat thoroughly enough to kill botulism spores, or because the temperature they would need to be heated to would produce an inedible end product. These foods include:

- highly viscous foods like peanut butter, pureed squash, or refried beans
- foods packed in oil, including canning oils or fats like lard
- dairy products like milk, cheese, or butter
- foods with flour, including breads
- foods containing corn starch—use Clear Jel instead for canning your own pie fillings

DEHYDRATING

Dehydrating is one of the oldest methods of food preservation. Removing moisture from foods through dehydration or drying can be used to preserve fruits, vegetables, meats, and herbs. Molds, yeasts, and bacteria need moisture to grow, so when foods are sufficiently dried, these microorganisms cannot grow and the food doesn't spoil. For food storage, dehydrating is a fantastic way to get a lot of nutrients into a little space. A full stalk of celery dehydrates to about one cup of dry celery.

Dehydrating Basics

For best results, follow these simple dehydrating guidelines:
- Use high-quality, fresh foods.

- Prepare your food in the size you would like it before dehydrating. If you want diced peppers, dice them before drying.
- Slice food as evenly as possible. Thin slices will dry faster than thick ones, and slicing thick or thin will be a personal preference, but uniform slice thickness helps the food all dry at the same rate.
- Drying times will be affected by the moisture in the air, so what could take six hours to dehydrate on a dry day may take ten hours in high humidity.
- The odor from strong-smelling foods will permeate the air and nearby drying trays when they are dehydrating. Apples dried in the dehydrator at the same time as onions will make onion-flavored apples. Foods with strong odors can also be dehydrated outdoors or in a shed to keep the house smelling nice.

DEHYDRATING METHODS
Solar
In order to dehydrate food, you'll need a method of drying it. The most primitive and least controllable method for dehydrating food is drying in the sun. To dry food in the sun, you need a hot sunny day with low humidity. Most foods will require more than one day to get sufficiently dry, so this method won't work in areas where there is insufficient sunshine or high humidity. The food should be protected from dirt and insects. Window screen is an excellent material to use above and below the foods you are dehydrating to provide this protection.

To shorten the drying time, use a solar dehydrator. These dehydrators amplify the heat from the sun while still allowing for air flow and moisture escape. Commercial solar ovens like the All American Sun Oven can be used as a solar dehydrator with the door of the oven slightly ajar. Instructions for building a simple solar dehydrator can be found online at **www.instructables.com/id/ Solar-Food-Dehydrator-Dryer**.

Conventional Oven
Most ovens can be used to dehydrate food. The oven temperature should be set between 120°F and 145°F (49°C and 63°C). Use an oven thermometer to test the temperature if you have an oven that just has a "warm" setting. Food will take a little longer to dry at lower temperatures, but also won't be as likely to scorch. Most gas ovens do not have a setting below 200° F (93°C). If you have an oven that will not heat to a low temperature, you may be able to use the heat of the oven light to dehydrate instead. Again, use an oven thermometer to check the internal temperature.

Once the temperature is set, prepare your food and put it on trays in the oven. Mesh trays work best, but baking sheets can also be used. To create more surface area for drying, stack multiple trays in the oven using spacers to maintain airflow across each tray.

Excalibur shelf-style dehydrator

Leave the oven door open a crack to let the moisture escape. You may need to prop it open with something. A fan can be used near the oven to increase airflow and decrease drying time.

Using an oven to dehydrate is not the most energy-efficient method of drying and also ties up your oven for the time the food is drying. It is, however, an inexpensive way to test out dehydrating and see how you like dried foods. If you find you like it, you'll probably want to purchase a dehydrator.

Food Dehydrator

There are two primary designs of food dehydrators on the market—stackable and shelf style. Stackable dehydrators are designed with individual trays that stack vertically on the dryer unit. Shelf-style dehydrators have shelves that can be slid in and out of a housing box like oven trays. Here's what you'll want to consider when you're purchasing a dehydrator.

Heat source location and air flow: Stackable dehydrators have their heat source and fan either at the top or bottom of the unit. The fan at the bottom is a more efficient design as heat rises; however, some of these stackable dehydrators have problems getting an even temperature to all the trays, requiring frequent tray rotation during the drying process. A bottom-mounted fan can also be difficult to clean if you are drying juicy items that can drip.

Some shelf-style dehydrators also have their heat source at the bottom, but a few have the heat and fan at the back of the dehydrator. A back-mounted fan allows the warm air to blow across the trays instead of up through them, providing more even heat across the trays as well as leaving the bottom of the dehydrator empty and easy to clean.

A few dehydrators don't use a fan at all, instead relying on convection heat to dry the foods. This design adds to the versatility of the dehydrator, allowing it to be used for various purposes including starting seeds and proofing yogurt;

Dehydrating Frozen Vegetables

Commercially packaged frozen vegetables were perfectly blanched prior to freezing and are ready to dehydrate right out of the package. Just pour them on the dehydrator tray frozen and dry until crisp. Slice larger vegetables like broccoli into thinner pieces to speed up the drying time.

however, food will take almost twice as long to dry in a convection-only dehydrator as opposed to a unit including a fan.

Durability: A cheap dehydrator can be just that—cheap. You don't want to be spending more money on another dehydrator because yours wasn't built to last. Most quality dehydrators come with a manufacturer's warranty and can still be drying foods ten or more years after purchasing them. Most dehydrators are made of food-grade plastic, but a few of the more expensive models are built with a stainless steel housing and racks.

Versatility: This is where the stackable dehydrators and shelf-style dehydrators really diverge. Stackable dehydrators can expand their drying area by adding more trays. However, they have a fixed space between trays, so they can only dry small items.

The shelf-style design can be used with some or all of the trays removed, allowing them to be used for drying bulkier items like broccoli and flowers, raising bread, and making yogurt. But if you run out of space with a shelf-style dehydrator, you'll need to purchase a whole new unit instead of just adding trays.

STORING DEHYDRATED FOODS

Dehydrated foods need to be stored in airtight containers, especially in humid environments. Mason jars or clean plastic food jars (like the kind that held peanut butter) with their lids screwed on tight work great for short-term storage. If you are planning on storing your dehydrated foods for longer than a few months, it is best to add an oxygen absorber to the jar or use a vacuum sealer with a jar sealer attachment to remove the oxygen from the jar. Dehydrated foods can also be stored in Mylar bags if they are not too sharp and the Mylar is at least 5 mil thick (see chapter six for more information on sealing food in Mylar bags). Sealing in thinner Mylar bags or vacuum sealer bags will usually result in the bag being punctured by the sharp edges of the dry food product.

Drying Fruits

Who doesn't love some good dried apples or fruit leather? Fruits are one of the tastiest and easiest food items to dehydrate. Most fruits can be dehydrated without pretreatment, although a few will produce a better end product with some pretreatment to preserve flavor or color. Fruits should be dried until they are leathery—about 10-20 percent moisture content—and are perfect for eating in their dried state. They can be reconstituted or used in baking as well.

FRUIT	PRETREATMENT	PRETREAT FOR COLOR RETENTION	DRYING TIME IN HOURS
Apples	Wash, slice, and core. Peeling is optional. Peels dry tough.	Yes	7 to 15
Apricots	Wash, cut in half or slices, remove pits.	Yes	20 to 28
Bananas	Peel and slice.	Recommended	6 to 10
Blueberries	Wash and remove stems. Dip in boiling water for 15 to 30 seconds to crack skins before drying.	No	7 to 15
Cherries	Wash, cut in half, remove pits. Place on trays skin side down.	No	13 to 21

MAKING FRUIT LEATHER

Fruit leathers are a great way to use soft or over-ripe fruit and are extremely easy to make. Puree the fruit in a food processor or blender, adding sugar, brown sugar, honey, or corn syrup for sweetener if desired. The granulated sugars may produce a less pliable finished leather than their liquid counterparts. If you have a commercial dehydrator, cover your dehydrator trays with custom fruit leather sheets or use plastic wrap—the press-to-seal type is really easy to work with and can be cut to fit round trays. Pour the fruit puree on the trays, a little thicker at the edges, and dry until it's leathery. If you get it too dry, just create some humidity by boiling dinner or doing some canning while

FRUIT	PRETREATMENT	PRETREAT FOR COLOR RETENTION	DRYING TIME IN HOURS
Grapes	Wash, remove stems. Dip in boiling water for 30 to 90 seconds to crack skins before drying.	No	22 to 30
Nectarines	Wash, cut into slices.	Recommended	8 to 16
Peaches	Wash, peel if desired by dipping in boiling water for one minute, then into cold water and slipping off skin. Slice.	Recommended	8 to 16
Pears	Wash and peel if desired. Remove stem and core. Slice.	Yes	20 to 36
Pineapples	Peel, core, and slice.	No	10 to 18
Plums	Wash, cut in half, and remove pits. Slice skin on the back side to speed drying.	No	22 to 30
Strawberries	Wash, cut off caps, and slice.	No	7 to 15

the fruit leather is still on the dehydrator trays, and it will soften back up. Roll and cut the leather to the size you like. Try different combinations of fruits and experiment with adding spices or flavored extracts before drying.

DRYING MEATS
Jerky

Make your own jerky by drying thin strips of raw meat. Jerky can be made with either slices of muscle or ground meat pressed flat by hand or through a jerky press. Use beef or game meats, like venison or elk, and trim any excess fat before processing. For meat slices, marinate or season the slices. If you are using

Drying Vegetables

Dehydrated vegetables make a great addition to soups or stews and can also be rehydrated and eaten as a side dish or meal. Most vegetables dry, store, and reconstitute better if they are blanched prior to drying. Picking a vegetable starts an enzyme reaction that changes the vegetable's taste and texture over time. Blanching slows or stops that enzyme reaction and also relaxes the tissue of the vegetable, creating a product that dries faster, keeps its color better, and rehydrates with better quality than its unblanched counterpart. Vegetables should be dried until they are crisp and snap when bent—about 5 to 10 percent moisture content.

VEGETABLE	PREPARATION	BLANCH	DRYING TIME IN HOURS
Beans (green)	Wash, remove stems, and slice.	3-4 minutes	8 to 12
Beets	Wash, trim tops, steam until tender. Cool, peel, and slice, cube, or shred.	No	8 to 12
Broccoli	Wash, cut into pieces, splitting stems.	2-3 minutes	10 to 14
Carrots	Wash and peel. Cut into slices or cubes.	Steam 3-4 minutes	6 to 10
Cauliflower	Wash, cut into pieces, splitting stems.	3-4 minutes	7 to 11
Celery	Wash and slice.	Optional; steam 2-3 minutes	3 to 10
Corn	Shuck, removing husk and silk.	2-3 minutes	6 to 10

ground meat, mix the seasonings in with the meat before flattening. Dry jerky six to ten hours at a temperature of at least 145°F (63°C). If your dehydrator does not dry at that high a temperature, precook your meat strips by submerging them in boiling water or 1:1 water/vinegar solution for 20 seconds before

VEGETABLE	PREPARATION	BLANCH	DRYING TIME IN HOURS
Greens (kale, lettuce, spinach, chard)	Wash, remove stems.	Optional; steam until wilted	3 to 7
Mushrooms	Wash in cold water and remove woody parts of stems. Slice down through the cap and stem.	No	3 to 7
Onions	Peel and cut in rings or chop.	No	4 to 8
Peas	Shell and wash.	Steam 3-4 minutes	4 to 8
Peppers	Wash, core, and slice or dice.	No	4 to 8
Potatoes	Wash, peel, and slice, dice, or shred.	Steam 4-6 minutes, then rinse in cool water	6 to 14
Tomatoes	Wash, remove stems. Peel if desired by dipping in boiling water for 30-60 seconds, then into cold water and slipping off skins. Slice large tomatoes or halve the cherry variety.	No	5 to 9
Zucchini	Wash, peel if desired, and slice or shred.	No	7 to 11

marinating and drying. Studies done by the University of Colorado recommend precooking all jerky prior to drying to reduce the risk of salmonella or *E. coli* infection. Jerky will keep for one to two months on the shelf or up to twelve months in the freezer. Vacuum sealing your jerky will extend the shelf life.

Dried Cooked Meats

Meats can also be dried after they are cooked and either eaten dry or reconstituted in a soup or stew. Cook the meat as you normally would. Smaller pieces dry better—the meat can be cut before or after it is cooked. Reconstitute the meat in boiling water.

FOODS THAT DON'T DEHYDRATE WELL

Most foods can be dried, but a few don't produce a very good end product. You may add to this list as you experiment with food dehydration, but here are some foods that produce a less than stellar end product:

- cucumbers
- lettuce
- radishes
- winter squash
- avocados
- citrus fruits
- melons
- berries like blackberries or raspberries

FREEZING

Storing food in your freezer is a common and simple way to preserve food. You probably have food in your freezer right now. Foods can be frozen individually or cooked into meals and frozen ready to heat and serve.

For best results freezing foods, follow these guidelines:

- Freeze foods while they are still fresh.
- Place foods in the freezer as quickly after packaging as possible.
- Freeze foods quickly by allowing air to flow around each package so it can freeze faster; don't stack unfrozen foods together in the freezer.
- Organize your freezer so you are using the oldest foods first.

Freezing sufficiently stops the enzymatic breakdowns in fruits, but vegetables should be blanched before freezing. Use the blanching times in the following table to prepare vegetables for freezing.

VEGETABLE	BLANCHING TIME IN BOILING WATER
Asparagus	2-4 minutes
Beans (green or wax)	2-4 minutes
Beets	Sufficiently heated in peeling process
Broccoli	3 minutes
Brussels sprouts	3 minutes
Cabbage	1½ minutes
Carrots	Small whole 5 minutes, sliced or diced 2 minutes
Cauliflower	3 minutes
Corn	4 minutes
Greens, beet greens, collards, kale, spinach	2-3 minutes
Mushrooms	Whole 5 minutes, slices 3 minutes
Onions	None
Peas	1½ minutes
Peppers	None
Potatoes	5 minutes
Pumpkin and winter squash	Cook until tender
Summer squash, zucchini, crookneck	3 minutes

Freezing keeps food safe to eat indefinitely, but the quality of the frozen food degrades over time. Air is the primary enemy to long-term storage of foods in the freezer, causing freezer burn and dehydration within a few months. To increase freezer storage times, pack your foods in a vacuum sealer bag like a FoodSaver bag. These bags, sealed with a vacuum sealer, reduce the air that can contact your foods and dramatically increase palatable storage times in a freezer. To get the best seal on foods with a lot of liquid in them or to preserve the shape of fragile foods like berries, freeze the foods first in serving-size containers, then remove from the container, vacuum seal the frozen food, and return it to the freezer.

SUMMARY

Canning, dehydrating, and freezing are excellent methods of preserving your own fresh foods, resulting in a more self-sufficient lifestyle and adding delicious foods to your short-term food storage.

6. PACKAGING DRY FOODS FOR LONG-TERM STORAGE

As soon as you have acquired dry foods for long-term storage, there are enemies that are working against you. If left unchecked, these enemies will steal nutrients and flavor, make your food taste foul, or render it entirely inedible. Don't let the enemies of food storage win! Proper packaging and storage methods can prevent these problems from ruining your efforts and your food. The last thing you want after investing time and money into food storage is to have it inedible when you need it.

In order to properly avoid the enemies of food storage, it's important to know what they are.

ENEMIES OF FOOD STORAGE

Temperature

Ideally, your food in long-term storage will be stored at temperatures between 50°F and 60°F (10°C and 16°C). Heat causes food quality, taste, and nutritional value to decline. A basement, crawl space, or root cellar all work well for keeping temperatures down. Be aware of possible moisture problems if using a crawl space or root cellar. In the absence of a basement, choose the coolest spot you can for your food storage. If you can't get a room down to 60°F (16°C), get it as cool as you can. Even 75°F (24°C) is better than 90°F (32°C). Plug heating ducts to the storage area if possible to keep it cool in the winter.

Light

Exposing food storage to light can cause deterioration of flavor, appearance, and nutrition. Sunlight compounds the problems by adding the effects of heat as well. Keep your food in opaque containers if possible. Containers that light can permeate, like PETE bottles, glass jars, and some buckets, should be stored in a dark room or covered to reduce light exposure.

Oxygen

Oxygen in contact with food causes oxidation, leading to flavor loss, discoloration, odor, and rancidity. The air we breathe is 20.95 percent oxygen. The ideal oxygen level for food storage is less than 1 percent. Using oxygen absorbers in airtight food storage containers can reduce the oxygen level to 0.1 percent or lower.

Moisture

Dried foods need a low moisture content to store well. Moisture aids the growth of bacteria and mold. Foods should always be stored in airtight containers that keep moisture out, especially in humid environments. Exterior sources of moisture, like direct contact with water, can cause rusting on some food storage cans, eventually making the food in them inedible. Storing cans

Eliminating Insects From Dried Foods

Insects, larvae, and eggs can be present in bulk foods before you purchase them. If the food is not treated to eliminate these pests, they can hatch and grow, feeding on your food and leaving a mess in their wake. Protect your food from insect infestation using one of these methods:

Oxygen Absorbers (Recommended)
Properly used, oxygen absorbers reduce the amount of oxygen in a container to 0.1 percent or less. This is insufficient oxygen for adult or larval insects and insect eggs, and they will be eradicated within fourteen days of sealing. Because oxygen absorbers are also the most reliable method of reducing oxygen in a container, by using them for insect control you are taking care of two problems at once.

Dry Ice
Dry ice is frozen carbon dioxide. Dry ice treatment is not recommended for removing oxygen for long-term storage, but it has been shown to be effective in eliminating adult insects and larvae. However, fumigating your food with dry ice isn't fully effective against eggs. To fumigate with dry ice, place 3 to 4 inches (8 to 10cm) of grain or other dried food at the bottom of a 5-gallon bucket. Add about

directly on concrete or other cold flooring can occasionally result in condensation buildup on the bottom side of the can. Food should always be stored so there is insulation between a hard floor and the food container.

Pests

Pests include rodents, insects in all their stages, and any other living thing that wants to eat your food. You didn't buy your food to feed pests, so take measures to keep them out of it. Keep food in containers that protect it from rodents or insects chewing through. Properly treat your bulk foods for possible insect egg or larva infestation prior to storage (see the Eliminating Insects From Dried Foods sidebar in this chapter).

Handling

Handling of food products is especially problematic with containers that are easily cracked or compromised. Glass jars break, plastics can crack, Mylar bags can develop pinhole leaks or tears, bucket seams and seals can leak, and even #10 cans can develop air leaks through rough handling.

2 ounces of crushed dry ice, and cover with the remaining food. Put the lid on loosely and wait for the dry ice to fully evaporate (around thirty minutes).

Freezing

Freeze 1 to 15 pounds (½ to 7kg) of food, double bagged in plastic, for two to three days. Freezing kills adult and larval insects but is not guaranteed effective against eggs. Thaw thoroughly and make sure the food is moisture free before storing it.

Diatomaceous Earth

Diatomaceous earth (DE) is a natural insecticide consisting of fossilized remains of diatoms, a hard-shelled algae. Under a microscope the fine powder looks like shards of glass. It does not harm humans, so is safe to ingest, but it will damage insects that come in contact with it so they die of desiccation (drying out). A small amount of DE mixed in with your dry food or placed in the bottom of a bucket will kill the insects that contact or ingest it. There is a lot of room for error with this method, as the insect actually has to contact the DE to be affected by it, so I would recommend another method of insect control in addition to or instead of using DE.

Time

Time is a food storage enemy we have little control over. It marches on regardless of how we try to slow it down. The best way to prevent food spoilage due to time is to rotate your storage foods, using the oldest foods first. This ensures that the foods you have stored will always be the freshest they can be.

PROTECTING FOOD STORAGE WITH OXYGEN ABSORBERS

Oxygen absorbers are small packets filled primarily with iron powder developed for reducing oxygen in a food storage package. When exposed to air, the iron in the packet oxidizes, using the oxygen in the atmosphere to chemically change to iron oxide (rust). When an oxygen absorber is working, the oxidation creates heat and the packet gets hot to the touch.

Oxygen absorbers are available in various sizes, each capable of absorbing a specified volume of oxygen, listed in cubic centimeters (cc). The size of oxygen absorber needed depends on the food you are storing and the size of container it is being stored in. Oxygen absorbers use oxygen from the void air space in a container. This is the space between the food particles. Foods like macaroni will have more void air space in a full container than foods like flour. There is some fancy math to figure out exactly how much oxygen is in a container of food and from there determine which size oxygen absorber to use. It is not as simple as it may seem—cubic centimeters, which is a measure of volume, does not convert neatly from a measure of weight like pounds without more information, like knowing the specific densities of each food you want to pack. Thankfully, there has been enough research on oxygen absorbers and food storage that instead of getting into advanced math, I can provide a simple table for reference. Combine oxygen absorbers if necessary to achieve the volume of absorption needed in your food container. For example, five 100 cc absorbers will do the same job as one 500 cc absorber.

FOOD TYPE	QUART POUCH	#10 CAN OR GAL-LON CONTAINER	5- OR 6-GALLON BUCKET
Powders—flour, powdered milk, pancake mix	50 cc	300 cc	1,000 cc
Small grains— rice, wheat, oats	50 cc	300 cc	1,500 cc
Beans	100 cc	500 cc	1,500 cc
Pastas	100 cc–200 cc	500 cc–700 cc	1,500 cc–2,000 cc

Oxygen absorbers

Food sealed in a #10 can

After being exposed to the air, oxygen absorbers are only viable for a limited amount of time. Oxygen absorbers are best used within thirty to sixty minutes of opening. You want as much of the iron powder to oxidize while sealed in your container as possible. Leave the oxygen absorbers in their original packaging until you are ready to use them. Fill all your containers, then open the package of oxygen absorbers, insert them into the containers, and seal the food storage container as quickly as possible. Any oxygen absorbers you will not use quickly need to be repackaged in an airtight container to stop oxidation and keep them good for later use. You can seal them into a vacuum sealer bag (like FoodSaver), Mylar bag, or tightly into a small canning jar with a tight-fitting lid, and they will be ready to use the next time you need to seal something. For convenience, repackage large quantities of oxygen absorbers into smaller packs using either a vacuum sealer bag or a Mylar bag.

LONG-TERM STORAGE OPTIONS
#10 Cans
Holding almost 1 gallon of food, #10 cans are one of these best ways to package and store dry foods.

Pros
- when sealed properly, they are impermeable to light and air
- cases stack well
- sturdy
- convenient size for most foods
- easy to use in rotation shelving

Cons

- difficult to find the sealing equipment and empty cans
- can sealers and empty cans are expensive for a single user
- can rust if exposed to moisture

In order to pack your food in a #10 can, you will need access to new cans and lids, oxygen absorbers, and a dry pack can sealer. Empty cans are lightweight, but having them shipped is costly due to their size and fragility when empty. The cost decreases if you can purchase a full pallet load. Dry pack can sealers start at around eight hundred dollars for a hand-crank version and thirteen hundred dollars for a motorized canner. If you want to purchase a can sealer and cans, it may be something you want to invest in with a few friends or relatives to reduce the cost.

Sealing Food in a #10 Can

1. Gather supplies. You'll need product, cans, lids, oxygen absorbers, can sealer, and some way to label the cans when they're sealed. You could make labels or just write on the can with a permanent marker.
2. Fill the cans with product until it is about ½ inch (1cm) from the top of the can.
3. Shake the cans or tap them on your work surface to settle the contents, then fill the rest of the can.
4. Add an oxygen absorber to the top of the can.
5. Place the lid on the can and seal following the instructions for the can sealer you are using.
6. Label and date the cans before storing them.

VACUUM SEALER BAGS

Some dry foods may be stored in vacuum sealer bags like FoodSaver bags. These bags are thin and clear, so they do not protect your food from light or most pests, and won't work if your product has any sharp edges, like pasta. Even if your food will not puncture the bag, it will need to be stored inside a barrel or bucket to protect the fragility of the bag and keep light out. Vacuum sealer bags are better used for foods stored in your freezer than for long-term storage.

Pros

- Sealers and bags are available at most big-box stores.
- Sealers can be used for vacuum sealing frozen foods, clothing for emergency kits, and dry food in mason jars.

Cons

- Thin bags are easily punctured by sharp-edged foods, rough handling, and rodents.
- Clear bags expose food to light.

MYLAR BAGS

Mylar is a brand name of metallized plastic pouches that are commonly used for long-term food storage. They are usually silver in color, but can come coated with other colors as well.

Pros

- readily available from online resellers
- inexpensive
- protect food from light and air
- various sizes available, plus you can create your own sizes by cutting and resealing them
- reusable

Cons

- not rodent-proof
- seal can be compromised if the bag puckers at the seal during sealing
- can puncture when sealing products with sharp edges, like pasta
- do not withstand rough handling

Mylar bags are available in a variety of thicknesses, most ranging

FoodSaver vacuum sealer

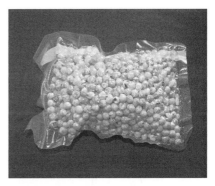

Freeze-dried peas sealed in a vacuum sealer bag

Food sealed in a Mylar bag, two empty Mylar bags of different sizes

Recycle for Free Mylar Bags

Many foods from the grocery store are packaged in Mylar bags that can be reused if they are opened carefully and washed out. You will find Mylar packaging primarily on snack foods like potato chips, cookies, or lining boxes of crackers or other snacks. These bags are thin, usually under the 4.5 mil recommended to use for food in long-term storage, so if you are going to use them, stick to soft foods like flour, and store the filled bags inside a bucket or other container to protect from light, abuse, and pests.

from 3.5 mil to 7 mil. A mil is one thousandth of an inch, so it's pretty thin, but there is quite a difference between 3.5 mil bags and 7 mil bags. The 3.5 mil bags are very thin and flexible—about the thickness of a potato chip bag. The 7 mil bags are much sturdier and less flexible. With the thinner bags, under 4.5 mil, there can be some light permeation. Thinner bags are also prone to being punctured by the foods being packaged or through rough handling. I recommend 4.5 mil or higher thickness for long-term food storage.

A few styles of Mylar bags are available with zip-seal tops. These bags still need to be sealed with a heat sealer above the zipper to ensure an airtight seal for storage. Use the zip seal to open and reseal the bag after it has been cut open for use.

Mylar bags can be reused after they are emptied. Just wash them out, let them thoroughly dry, and they're ready to fill and seal again. If you plan to reuse bags, you'll get the best results by cutting the bag open just under the seal and then resealing the bag as close to the top as possible. Give your bags a thorough check for holes or tears prior to reusing them.

Sizes of Mylar bags range from 5 gallon to small enough for a packet of seeds. If you can't find the size you need, you can always make your own custom-sized bags from larger bags. Use scissors to cut the large bag to the size you want and seal the open edges, leaving one side open for filling.

Sealing Food in a Mylar Bag

1. Gather your supplies. You'll need product, bags, oxygen absorbers, and a method of sealing the bag.
2. Fill the bag with product. Allow enough room at the top that the bag can close around the food without puckering.
3. Add oxygen absorbers suitable for the size of package you are sealing.

4. If necessary, wipe the inside of the bag opening with a dry rag to remove any food particles that may prevent a good seal.
5. Seal the bag using one of the following heat-sealing options.
6. Label and date the bag before storing. Store Mylar bags in a bucket, tote, barrel, or other container to protect them from damage and pests.

Mylar Sealing Options

Commercial impulse sealer: Impulse sealers are made specifically for sealing Mylar bags. They are available in a variety of sizes and styles and are available for as low as fifty dollars for a 12-inch (30cm) sealer. These sealers are easy to use, and the amount of heat they generate is perfect for sealing Mylar bags.

Vacuum sealer with heat strip: The heat strip that seals vacuum sealer bags can be used to seal Mylar as well. If your sealing strip is thin, you may want to seal it two or three times slightly offset to make sure the seal is sufficient for the pressure created by the oxygen absorber.

Clothing iron: To use a clothing iron, set your iron to the cotton or high setting and turn the steam off. In order to have the pressure necessary to seal the bag, you'll need something rigid underneath the bag you're ironing. For sealing edges on a newly cut, empty bag, the top of your ironing board covered with a clean cloth will work for support. Once the bag is full, you won't be able to lay it down without spilling the contents, so use a thin board or metal bar that can be laid across the open end of the bag at least ½ inch (13mm) in from the edge. Fold the top of the bag over the support and iron it closed.

Hair straightener: Good for more than just style, hair straighteners are an inexpensive and easy way to get Mylar bags sealed. These hair-styling tools have two flat hot plates that clamp together and can be bought new for as little as ten dollars. They aren't very long, so you may need to press to seal more than once across the top of the bag. If you're buying a hair straightener just for sealing bags, the straighteners with thinner plates are sufficiently wide.

BUCKETS

Plastic HDPE (high-density polyethylene) buckets are available in sizes from 2 gallons to 6 gallons, either round or square, and are a great method of storing bulk foods.

Pros
- hold a large amount of food
- handles make them easy to carry

- stack well
- sturdy
- can be used in conjunction with various sizes of Mylar bags

Cons

- can get heavy depending on the size of bucket and type of stored food
- some gas permeability—buckets containing food should not be stored in areas with strong odors or fumes like garages
- plastic can become brittle over time, especially if subjected to wide temperature variations

When storing food in buckets, start with buckets that are clean, food grade, and have never stored products other than foods (like paint or oil). Food-grade buckets will have recycle code 2, but not all HDPE buckets with code 2 are food grade. Purchase new buckets that are labeled as food-grade buckets, or buy used buckets that have been used only for storing food. If in doubt about whether a bucket is food grade, assume it is not and use it for a nonfood purpose. Buckets can be obtained for around seven dollars new or can be found used at locations like bakeries and restaurants for little or no cost. Make sure any bucket you are going to use for storing food has a good sealing lid with it. This may mean buying new lids for the used buckets if their lids don't seal well or are missing the gasket.

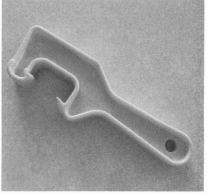

Gamma Seal lid on a bucket   **Bucket opener tool**

Bucket Lids

Standard bucket lids snap onto the bucket top and need to be pried off one wing at a time when you want to open the bucket. A rubber mallet can be used to seal and reseal the lid on the bucket, or you can stand on the lid and stomp around the edges to snap it on (with shoes on, of course!). Using a bucket opener tool makes removing the lids much easier than trying to take them off with your fingers. Bucket opener tools can be purchased at food storage retailers and are well worth the three-dollar price tag if you have any of your food storage in buckets.

An alternative to a standard bucket lid is a Gamma Seal lid. These can be useful if you plan on opening a specific bucket and closing it back up often. The Gamma Seal lid is a two-part lid consisting of an outer ring that snaps onto the bucket and an inner lid that screws into the outer ring—no stomping or mallet required to reseal the lid. These lids cost more than a standard lid, so if you have a lot of buckets, you may want to put them only on the buckets you'll be accessing the most. Once a Gamma Seal lid is installed on a bucket, it does not come off. But you can always refill the bucket and continue using the lid.

Lining Buckets

Buckets are made of HDPE plastic. This plastic is porous, although microscopically so, and over time gas can permeate your bucket. Some buckets are also slightly translucent, allowing light to penetrate to the food stored inside. For extra protection from permeability and light, or to use a nonfood-grade bucket for storing food, line the bucket with a large Mylar bag before filling it with food. The Mylar gives an extra layer of protection from air and light as well as keeps your food together if your bucket is broken for any reason.

Buckets—They're Not Just for Food

Buckets are a very versatile container for more preparedness purposes than just storing food.

- organize other dry storage items like toiletries, medical supplies, matches, or canning supplies in them
- pad the lid and use it as a seat
- use it for a step stool
- haul water
- store or haul animal feed
- store seeds
- add a seat and make a toilet (use waste collection bags to be more sanitary)
- hold fish, clams, or crawfish you've caught
- collect produce from your garden
- hold supplies like an emergency kit or extra food for evacuation

Sealing Food in a Bucket

1. Gather your supplies. You'll need product, buckets, and lids. Bucket-sized Mylar bags are optional.
2. If using a Mylar bucket liner, place the liner in the bucket.
3. Fill the bucket or liner with product.
4. Add appropriate-sized oxygen absorbers.
5. If using a Mylar bucket liner, seal the liner with one of the heat sources previously mentioned.
6. Add the lid and snap it down.
7. Label the bucket with the product and date before storing. You can use a label, write on tape, or write directly on the bucket with a permanent marker.

CANNING JARS

Dry foods can be sealed in canning jars for long-term storage using either an oxygen absorber or a vacuum sealer with a jar lid sealing attachment. Do not use the vacuum sealer attachment to seal wet foods in jars—always use approved canning techniques as outlined in chapter five of this book.

Pros

- impermeable to air and moisture
- easy to find
- versatile

Cons

- small volume
- light penetrable
- heavy and prone to breakage

Sealing Dry Food in a Canning Jar With an Oxygen Absorber

1. Gather your supplies. You'll need product, jars, two-piece caps including rings and new lids, and oxygen absorbers.
2. Fill the jars with product.
3. Add an oxygen absorber.
4. Wipe the top of the jar with a dry cloth if there is any residue from filling the jar that may interfere with the seal.
5. Place the lid on the jar and tighten it on with the ring.
6. Label and date your jars before storing.

Bottle Up Some Variety

Vacuum sealing foods in jars does not have to end with rice and beans. Removing the oxygen from the atmosphere inside the jar will prevent oxidation and rancidity in a variety of foods. Try sealing these foods in jars with an oxygen absorber or vacuum sealer to increase their shelf life:

- crackers
- chocolate (candy bars and chocolate chips)
- nuts
- shredded coconut
- cooking oils
- solid fats like lard
- dried fruits and vegetables
- herbs and spices
- dry ingredients for coffee and tea

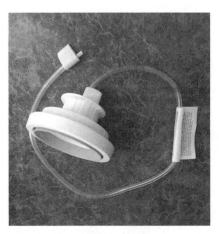

FoodSaver jar sealer attachment

Food stored in reused PETE plastic containers

Sealing Dry Food in a Canning Jar With a FoodSaver Jar Sealer Attachment

1. Gather your supplies. You'll need product, jars, new lids but not rings, a vacuum sealer, and the jar sealer attachment including the connector hose.
2. Fill the jars with product.
3. Check the rims of the jars and clean off any residue that may inhibit a good seal.
4. If you are packaging powdery foods, place an inverted cupcake paper between the food and the lid to keep the vacuum from sucking the food through the sealing surface.
5. Place the lid on the jar.
6. Make sure the jar sealer is attached properly to the vacuum sealer and place it over the lid.
7. Activate the vacuum sealer and allow it to seal until the lid seals to the jar. You'll hear the vacuum sound change when it's done.
8. Label and date your jars before storing.

PETE PLASTIC CONTAINERS

Many foods that can be purchased at the store are packaged in PETE plastic containers. This plastic has recycle code 1 and is stamped with the letters PETE or PET next to the code. Most of these containers are clear or translucent, so store them away from light to better protect the foods in them. Once a PETE container is emptied of its original contents, wash it out and allow it to thoroughly dry before storing food in it.

Pros

- practically free
- smaller containers work great for food items you only have a small amount of

Cons

- small
- light penetrable
- may get cracked or damaged with rough handling

Sealing Food in PETE Containers

1. Gather your supplies. You'll need product, clean and dry PETE containers, and oxygen absorbers.
2. Fill the containers with product. Some containers, like 2-liter soda bottles, have small mouth openings that will limit the size of food you can store in them. You may also find it helpful to use a funnel when filling, depending on the container opening size.
3. Add an oxygen absorber.
4. Check the openings of the containers and wipe off any residue that may inhibit a good seal.
5. Screw the lids on tight.
6. Label and date the containers before storing them.

SUMMARY

Your long-term storage may use a variety of these storage methods, depending on the food being stored and the resources available to you. Proper packaging and storage of your food will protect it from the enemies of food storage and ensure your food is as nutritious and great tasting as possible when you need to eat it.

7. BUYING FOOD

Having food storage actually provides your family with a large degree of budget flexibility. If a month is tight, you can use some of the food storage to feed your family until the next paycheck. But to do that, you first need to have some food storage, which usually means buying at least part of it. Most of us can only grow and preserve a small portion of our own food storage. Whatever cannot be produced yourself will need to be purchased.

FINDING THE MONEY

There's no doubt that food storage is an investment. A three- (or more) month supply of food is expensive. Sometimes it's tough just paying for all your typical monthly expenses, so how can you finance your food storage? First, do not go into debt to purchase your food storage. With prudence, you can purchase your long-term food storage without spending money you don't have. Here are some ideas to help you find money to buy food storage.

Lump-sum payments. If you get a tax return, inherit money from great-uncle Henry, get a bonus at work, are gifted money for your birthday or a holiday, or come upon a lump sum of money from some other source, use a portion or all of that money for food storage. These are great times to buy both food and the big-ticket preparedness items you want, like a grain grinder or solar oven.

Sell stuff. Hold a yard sale or sell products online to raise some extra money. You might be surprised what other people will pay for things you don't use or could do without. Be careful using online auction sites because you don't want the fees to eat up too much of your profits.

Save loose change. Drop the extra change in your pockets into a jar or other container at the end of each day. It doesn't take long for this to add up to more than just pocket change.

Quit buying stuff. Sometimes we make comfort purchases like eating lunch out or buying more shoes than we need. Next time you're tempted to buy something you could do without, set that money aside for food storage instead. Keep a master list of times you intentionally forfeit purchasing something in order to save for food storage. That way you have a tangible record of the money you've saved (see the Saving Through Sacrifice Worksheet). Also don't pay for things you can borrow like books and movies. The amount you'll be able to save will depend on your current shopping habits, of course, but even saving twenty dollars per month will add up in food over time.

After you have determined where the money is coming from, let's look at some options for purchasing food storage and how to best use the money you have available to you.

ONE LARGE PURCHASE

If you have the funds, making one large purchase to establish the bulk of your food storage is a great idea. Many food storage suppliers have package deals for one, three, six, or twelve month supplies of food that earn you a discount on that food as opposed to purchasing it one can at a time. When considering purchasing a food package, here are some questions to ask:

1. How many calories per day does the package provide? Calorie counts help you compare prices on various packages from different suppliers. You'll also want a calorie count high enough to sustain your activity level. Lower calorie levels could be purchased if you are supplementing the package with other foods.

2. Is the package comprised of individual ingredients or pre-packaged meals? Which do you want? Pre-packaged meals are very convenient, but ingredients allow you to mix up your own favorite meals and you're not locked into the same ten meals over and over.

3. Is it freeze-dried, dehydrated, or some of both? Freeze-dried will re-constitute faster and frequently retains better flavor and texture than dehydrated foods. Dehydrated foods tend to be less expensive.

4. Does the package include items my family cannot or will not eat? Remember, food allergies or personal tastes can substantially alter your family's food storage plan.

5. How is it packaged? Is it mostly #10 cans? Buckets? Pouches? Which can you store best at your house, and which is a size you can use quickly

Savings Through Sacrifice Worksheet

Use this worksheet to help keep track of funds you can use for food storage purchases instead of other items. Find a blank version in the appendix and online at **www.livingreadyonline.com/foodstorage**. Be very diligent about recording the money you save when you make a conscious effort to forgo something with the intention of saving for food storage.

Money Needed for Food Storage Purchases: _____

Item or Service Not Purchased	Savings Earned
_____	_____
_____	_____
_____	_____
_____	_____
_____	_____
_____	_____
_____	_____
_____	_____
_____	_____

TOTAL: _____

enough after opening? Some food in pouches does not have as long a shelf life as the same food stored in cans or buckets. Pouches can also be compromised by rodents or rough handling.

6. What is the shelf life? This is usually dependent on the packaging.
7. If the package includes meat, is it real meat or textured vegetable protein (TVP)? TVP is a soy-based meat substitute. Some people like the flavor and texture of it, and others don't. TVP is less expensive and has a shorter shelf life than freeze-dried meats.
8. Does the package include anything other than food? Some kits include extras like a stove, water, or fire-starting supplies. If you don't need

those items, they are an added expense, but if you do need them, having them included in the kit might be the least expensive way to get them.

The deciding factors in a food package purchase will depend on your own family's needs and circumstances.

An alternative to purchasing a preassembled kit is to determine the different foods and the amounts of each you will need and put together your own bulk purchase. There may be a preassembled kit that you can add to or change items out of to get the combination of food you need. Depending on what you want in your storage, your own large purchase might be a number of smaller purchases from a variety of suppliers including grocery stores and warehouse stores.

MONTHLY BUDGETED PURCHASES

Most of us can't purchase our food all at once and need to acquire it a little at a time. One way to do this is by setting a portion of your budget aside every month for food storage. Use that money to purchase extra nonperishable foods at the store or to make a purchase of other products you may need.

Some food storage companies have creative ways to help you purchase long-term food storage using a monthly budget. Food Insurance will allow you to purchase a package and then pay for it a month at a time. When a payment is received, a portion of the total food package is sent until you have paid for and received the entire package.

Thrive Life has a monthly purchase system they call the Thrive Q. This program allows you to add all the products you want to a list, set a budget and ship date, and then they ship items from your list up to your budget amount each month.

Check with the company you would like to purchase from to see if they have an automatic monthly payment program. If not, you can always schedule your own day each month for food storage shopping.

EXTRA-CAN METHOD

One extremely simple and budget-friendly way to build your food storage is the Extra-Can Method. Do your grocery shopping as usual and purchase an extra can or package of items you are buying anyway. It might only be an additional five to ten dollars every time you go shopping to get a few extra items. When you unload the groceries, those extra items go to your food storage, and before long you'll have a substantial stash of food for your family. If you are using the Menu Method for planning your food storage, you can easily identify a few extra ingredients that you can purchase during each shopping trip. If you have the extra money, you could purchase one full meal each shopping trip.

A variation on this method is to check your cupboards before your next shopping trip. Anything nonperishable that you were planning to eat and didn't is now food storage. That leftover jar of spaghetti sauce or can of green beans just helped your food storage grow. You probably have some food storage in the back of your pantry already!

SALES

Almost everything goes on sale some time. Even food. Your local grocery store probably has weekly specials. If any of those specials are foods that you want in your food storage, buying them on sale can save you a lot of money over the course of building your food storage. Don't limit yourself to sales on canned and dry foods. Fresh foods like produce and meat on sale can be bottled, dried, or frozen for storage.

In some areas, stores will have sales where you get a discount if you purchase a full case of one product at a time. These "case lot sales" are usually an excellent time to purchase canned vegetables and fruits as well as peanut butter, tuna, and chicken by the case. One benefit of purchasing a case is that you also get the box to store and transport the cans in, which can help with organizing your food storage.

Long-term food storage products also go on sale. Most food storage companies offer monthly specials either in store or online. Some even have occasional site-wide sales. To keep up with what is on sale at your favorite retailer, sign up for their online newsletters or follow them on social media. Some also have printed catalogs that arrive in the mail, and I'm sure they'd love to have you on their mailing list. Especially watch for deep discounts in September for National Preparedness Month and online sales for Black Friday and Cyber Monday in November.

Emergency Essentials offers group buys on specific products each month. With these sales, you need to purchase a specific quantity of the item to get the sale price. Sometimes the group buy is food products, and other times it is other preparedness items. Get some friends or family members to join with you on these group buys and you can usually get a nice discount off retail. Other companies may be willing to offer a discount for a group purchase as well.

Another place to find food storage products on sale is at preparedness events and expos. These take place across the country, and retailers at the expo often have their products available at special pricing. Know the regular price of products you are shopping for so you'll know if you are getting a good deal at the event.

Seasonal and Event Sales

In most stores, there is a predictable pattern for items that go on sale throughout the year. Remember, perishables like meats can be bottled or frozen for storage, and after some holidays seasonal items could go on clearance for even less. Here are a few to watch for:

- January: Super Bowl—Snacks, chips, soda, chicken wings
- February: National Canned Food Month—Canned fruits, vegetables, soups, and meats; Valentine's Day—Chocolates and candies
- March: St. Patrick's Day—Corned beef; National Frozen Food Month—All things frozen
- April: Easter—Eggs, ham
- May: Cinco de Mayo—Salsa, enchilada and taco sauces, tortillas; Memorial Day—Picnic supplies, grilling meats, condiments, charcoal
- June: National Dairy Month—Milk, cheese, eggs, other dairy products
- July: Fourth of July—Picnic supplies, grilling meats, condiments, charcoal
- August: Back to school—Tissues, lunch box foods great for emergency kits like pudding cups, granola bars, and juice pouches; Canning season—Sugar, pectin, corn syrup, pickling mixes, canning supplies
- September: Labor Day—Grilling meats, picnic supplies, condiments, charcoal
- October: Apples; Halloween—Chocolate and other candy, pumpkin
- November: Thanksgiving—Baking supplies, pie fillings, flavored gelatin, turkey, ham, boxed stuffing mix, canned olives, pickles
- December: Christmas—Baking supplies, turkey, ham, candy, oranges

COUPONS

You don't need to be an extreme couponer or stock up on preservative-rich foods you'll never eat to use coupons to help build your food storage. You don't even need to subscribe to a Sunday paper, although if you already do, you'll have a ready supply of coupons to use each week. Using coupons doesn't have to be difficult or too time-consuming. Here are some tips for using coupons for food storage.

1. Subscribe to preferred shopper programs at your favorite stores. These programs allow you to earn store credit on the purchases you are already making. That credit can be used to purchase food for your storage. It's like a coupon for money off that doesn't specify the products you have to buy.
2. Use coupon sites like Coupons.com and Redplum.com to print coupons for products you need to purchase.
3. Visit the websites and social media pages of brands you frequently buy—lots of times there are printable coupons available on their site or Facebook page.
4. Couple coupons with sales for added savings.
5. Free up money for food storage by using coupons to save on purchases of other products you normally buy.
6. Coupons are frequently available for cleaning products and personal care items like toothpaste and deodorant. Use those coupons to round out the nonfood items in your emergency supplies.
7. Use your manners. Don't clear the shelf of every coupon item the store has in stock. You can always visit another store or come back another day.

BULK PURCHASES

Purchasing food in bulk almost always gets you a better price than buying small packages. Some food storage retailers like Honeyville Grain will sell grains and flours in bulk packages of 25 or 50 pounds (11 or 23kg). You can also purchase food in bulk at warehouse stores like Sam's Club or Costco and some grocers. Large packaging is not always the best option. Oil, for instance, is better stored in smaller packaging with its original seal intact.

Most foods purchased in bulk are not sold in packaging that is suitable for long-term storage. Paper bags allow air to contact your food and are easily penetrated by rodents or infested with insects. Repackage these foods into long-term storage containers like cans, buckets, or Mylar bags after bringing them home.

FOOD CO-OPS

When a group of people get together to purchase food in bulk, they can form a food co-op. Each member of the co-op pays a specified amount and receives a portion of the total food purchased. Many times the food offered through the co-op is produced locally as well. These co-ops can have excellent pricing on quality items that can be canned or preserved.

Food Stamps for Food Storage?

Over 47 million American families use the federal Supplemental Nutrition Assistance Program (SNAP, or "food stamps") for at least a portion of their groceries. And 8 million more receive food assistance from WIC (Women, Infants, and Children). If your family has come on hard times and is using food assistance programs, it doesn't mean you can't add to your food storage. If your allotted assistance amount provides more than you eat in the month, set that extra aside as food storage. Many storage-friendly foods like rice, oats, peanut butter, and canned or dry beans can be purchased through the government food assistance programs.

NOT BUYING FOOD

It is possible to get food extremely cheap and even sometimes without paying for it at all. Try some of these ideas:

Trade for Food

This probably won't work at a supermarket, but it might at a farmers market or with a local grower. If you have a skill that could benefit them like fixing their machinery or cleaning equipment, offer to trade your help for food.

Gleaning

Some farms or orchards have an organized gleaning program that allows people to pick food that was missed during harvesting. Sometimes a portion is donated to a local food bank, other times the amount of produce you collect is yours to keep. At a farm or orchard without an organized gleaning program, you may be able to volunteer assistance at harvest time in exchange for a portion of the produce either free or at a discount.

Late Produce

Check farmers markets late in the day or grocery store produce departments for food they are going to discard. You may be able to get it at a highly discounted rate or even free. It won't be the best looking, but even wrinkly soft apples can be dehydrated or made into applesauce.

Grow a Garden

While not exactly free (seeds and bedding plants have a nominal cost), gardening is an extremely low-cost option for acquiring food. Tomatoes, onions, squash, beans, and peas are all easy to grow and produce a lot of food. Some communities have organized community gardens. Get involved in one if you don't have your own piece of dirt to grow in. If you don't have a garden but live near someone who does, let him know you are looking for food and are willing to work in exchange for some of the harvest. Use this same method with a neighbor who has fruit trees. Just putting the word out that you would like to can fruit and are willing to pick it yourself might land you some of her excess. I have both received and shared loads of extra garden produce through the years.

Hunt

Hunting has a cost associated with it in equipment, license fees, and travel, but it can provide fresh, natural meat for a fraction of the cost of purchasing meat at the store. Processing and packing it yourself instead of taking it to a packaging plant to be cut and wrapped saves even more. Be sure to check local regulations before planning your hunt.

SUMMARY

There are many options for purchasing your food storage, and none of them are the one right way. Each family has its own needs and budget, so use the buying options that work for you. The important thing is that you take the steps that will get food in your storage.

8. MAINTAINING BALANCE AND VARIETY

When my husband and I first started a serious food storage plan, we figured out how much white rice we would need if white rice was all we had to eat every day for a year. Then we bought that much rice, planning to add other foods to our storage later. I do not recommend you do this. First, it was a crazy amount of rice. More than fifteen years later we are still eating that rice. But most important, what kind of nutrition balance do you get from eating one food exclusively for long periods of time? Or even three or four of the same foods over and over? You want a well-rounded food storage plan that includes a variety of foods. Planning for and storing a range of different foods can provide your family with proper nutrition and reduce appetite fatigue. This chapter explains how to incorporate the various food groups into your food storage so you can maintain a balanced diet that has enough variety to meet your nutritional needs as well as your taste preferences. Use the My Family's Dietary Needs and Preferences worksheet in the appendix (or download it from **www.livingreadyonline.com/foodstorage**) to customize your food storage to include the balance and variety your family needs and wants.

STORING PROTEIN

Meats, beans, nuts, and other sources of protein provide bulk and essential nutrients, and are easy to include in any food storage plan.

Meat

One of the most common sources of protein in most diets is meat, and there are several options for getting meat in your food storage.

Freeze it. Meat in the freezer has a shelf life of six to twelve months. Sealed with a vacuum sealer, the shelf life can be extended up to three to five years (based on my own personal experience). Freezing meat is an excellent and inexpensive option for short-term food storage. But if the power goes out for an extended period of time, the frozen meat will need to be cooked and eaten quickly or preserved by drying or canning so it does not go bad.

Dry it into jerky. Or purchase jerky. Depending on how it's packaged (and how many preservatives are in the commercial kind), jerky has a shelf life of six to eighteen months. That is, if you can keep it hidden, because you know if jerky is hanging around where family members can find it, it won't last long at all. Another option is to preserve the meat by smoking it or curing it. There are many books available on both smoking and curing meat including *Cured* by Lindy Wildsmith.

Purchase commercially canned meats. These include canned meats like chicken, tuna, salmon, and other seafood. You can also purchase canned bacon, beef, pork, and of course SPAM. Some of these meats are really good, and others are highly processed. Check labels and try them out before stocking up on a lot of something you may end up not liking. Shelf life on commercially canned meats varies but averages about five years. Commercially canned products containing meat, like spaghetti sauce, soups, chili, and ravioli, can also be a way to store meat.

Bottle your own meat. Home-canned meat is shelf stable, precooked, and if it is properly stored, has a shelf life of up to two years. You can bottle game meat, beef, pork, chicken, turkey, and even fish. See chapter five for more information on canning meats.

Purchase freeze-dried meats. Freeze-dried meats are flash frozen, then put into a vacuum chamber to remove the moisture. When rehydrated, they retain the flavor and texture of fresh cooked meat. They are a little more expensive than some of the other options, but have a shelf life of twenty-five years. Chicken, turkey, beef, ground beef, sausage, and ham are all available in freeze-dried form.

Keep livestock. You can keep small animals like rabbits, chickens, and other poultry even on a small plot of land. If you have the room, consider larger animals like cows, sheep, goats, or pigs.

Stock the means to hunt, trap, or fish for meat. You'll need proper firearms and ammunition or archery equipment for hunting, appropriate-sized traps or snares for trapping, and fishing hooks, poles, and gear for fishing. We'll cover both livestock and wild game in more depth in chapter nine.

Textured Vegetable Protein

TVP is an acronym for textured vegetable protein, also occasionally called textured soy protein (TSP) or soy meat. High in fiber and low in fat, TVP provides a comparable percentage of protein per serving when reconstituted as meat.

But TVP is not meat. TVP is made from soy flour after the soy oil has been extracted. The flour is mixed with water, cooked under pressure, squirted out of a machine, and dried. The TVP fluffs with air pockets when it comes out of the extruder, giving it a texture and mouth feel similar to meat. TVP can be dried in various forms like strips, flakes, and crumbles, depending on what the final product will be used for.

In its natural state, TVP is tasteless, so most TVP packed for food storage has flavor added like chicken, ham, beef, taco, or bacon. You might be familiar with at least one form of TVP—artificial bacon bits—that can be found at most salad bars.

Eggs

Containing about 6 grams of protein each, eggs are another great source of protein in your food storage. They are also a key ingredient in many baking recipes. Eggs can be stored either fresh, powdered, or freeze-dried.

Fresh eggs. Keeping chickens, ducks, or other egg-laying poultry will provide a nearly continuous supply of fresh eggs. When an egg is laid, it has a coating called the bloom that helps prevent air from permeating the shell and lengthens the storage life of the egg. The bloom is removed when the egg is washed, so most eggs no longer have the bloom to protect them from air. One way to extend the shelf life of eggs is to create a replacement for the bloom by coating the eggshell with a thin layer of mineral oil. Oiled chicken eggs can store in cool temperatures for up to four months. Crack the stored eggs into a separate bowl to check for signs of spoilage before adding them to your food.

Powdered eggs. Powdered eggs are available from most major food storage companies. A #10 can of powdered eggs holds the equivalent of approximately 215 eggs. Powdered eggs can be substituted for fresh eggs in cooking or baking. They have one of the shortest shelf lives of any commercial dry food storage product, lasting only up to seven years.

Freeze-dried eggs. Freeze-dried precooked eggs are also available. These are eggs that have been cooked (usually scrambled) and then commercially freeze-dried. When rehydrated, they will only be cooked eggs and cannot be used as a raw egg or in baking.

Grow Your Own Dry Beans

Growing dry beans in your garden is super simple. It is best to know before-hand if you have a bush or a climbing variety so you can plant them in an area that will support their growth habit. Then plant the beans, water and weed them, and don't pick them until the pods are fully dry. If you are facing a freeze before your beans dry, pull the entire bean plant and hang or lay it in a well-ventilated area until the pods dry. Once the pods are dry, you can crack them open by hand or place them between two layers of fabric (old sheets work well) and beat or step on the pile to break the pods and free the beans. Then use a blow dryer or air compressor to blow the chaff off the top of the pile; your beans will have fallen to the bottom. If any are soft, let them air dry before storing. Freezing the dry beans for three days prior to storage will kill any eggs or larvae of pests like the bean weevil.

Beans

Beans combined with a cereal grain like corn, wheat, or rice are a complete protein source. Options for storing beans include precooked or dry beans.

Canned, wet pack. Various precooked beans are available at grocery stores either plain or in baked beans or chili. These beans are best for your short-term or mid-range food storage.

Dry beans. For a longer shelf life, store dry beans. Dry beans come in many varieties and can be cooked or ground into flour. They can be purchased pre-canned from food storage suppliers or in bulk from a grocery store. Properly stored, dry beans have a shelf life of thirty years.

Nuts and Peanut Butter

Nuts and peanut butter are best for shorter term food storage. Because of the oils they contain, they will go rancid quickly if not stored properly and rotated into your regular eating.

Nuts. For best success storing nuts, store whole, unsalted nuts in their shells. Unshelling nuts shorten their storage life. Nuts can be stored in a mason jar sealed with a vacuum sealer or in the freezer to extend their shelf life to approximately one year.

Peanut butter. Peanut butter is a great mid-range storage food. Peanut butter stores well for two to three years on the shelf. All-natural peanut butters will have a shorter shelf life. You can also get peanut butter powder from some food storage companies with a shelf life of three years.

Protein is also available in some vegetables like broccoli, cauliflower, and spinach, so if you don't have meat, beans, eggs, or nuts in your storage, you can still get protein from some of your veggies!

STORING DAIRY

Rich in calcium, dairy foods are an important part of our diets. Dairy includes many of the perishable items that you may think you can't have in your long-term food storage, like milk, yogurt, and cheeses.

Milk

Used for drinking and baking, as well as being the basis for making cheeses and yogurt, milk is a food storage staple that can be stored in a variety of ways.

Canned liquid milk products. Canned sweetened condensed and evaporated milk store well on the shelf for about a year, making them good candidates for short-term food storage. They will turn dark and develop an off flavor if kept too long past their expiration dates, which will be printed on their packaging.

Instant powdered nonfat milk. Instant powdered milks are available in grocery stores and from most major food storage manufacturers. In general, instant powdered milks mix easier into water and have a slightly better flavor than their non-instant counterparts. They also usually require more powder per gallon or liter to mix. This means you'll need to store a larger amount of powder with instant powdered milk than regular powdered milk to make the

Tips for Mixing Powdered Milk

Some instant powdered milk can stir right into cold water, but most dry milks (even some brands of instant milk) need a little encouragement in order to fully combine with water. To make mixing easier, try these tips:

- Mix with warm water.
- Use a whisk.
- Use a blender.
- Mix the dry powder into about one-fourth the total amount of water called for. After it is blended well, add the rest of the water.

same amount of liquid milk. This is not always true, depending on the brand, so check the powder-to-water mix ratio before purchasing.

Non-instant or regular powdered nonfat milk. Regular powdered milk is available from some food storage manufacturers. It is usually less expensive than the instant powders, but more difficult to mix with water. Either of the nonfat varieties have a shelf life of twenty years.

Whole milk powder. Powdered whole milk is also available under brand names like Néstle Nido. This milk has the most true-to-liquid flavor, but due to the fats present in the powder, it only has a one-year shelf life compared to the twenty-year shelf life of nonfat powdered milk. Whole milk powder could be a good option for a short-term food supply if it is rotated regularly.

Milk alternatives. A couple of food storage companies offer powdered milk alternatives. These products look like powdered milk, but generally have a better mouth feel and flavor. They are not 100 percent milk, but instead are made from a mix of other ingredients that can include whey, partially hydrogenated vegetable oil, corn syrup solids, coconut oil, or sugar. Check labels to know whether you are purchasing a 100 percent milk powder or a milk alternative.

Own a dairy animal. Having a large dairy animal like a cow or goat can be a sustainable source of fresh dairy for your food storage if you have space and feed available. We will discuss livestock in more depth in chapter nine.

Yogurt

Besides being full of healthy probiotics, yogurt can be a fresh substitute for sour cream or eaten for breakfast or a snack. Here are a couple of ways to get this perishable food into your food storage.

Freeze-dried yogurt. Available from a growing number of food storage suppliers, and incidentally, also in the baby food aisle of most grocers, freeze-dried yogurt bites make a fantastic snack and can also be reconstituted. In flavors like pomegranate, vanilla, strawberry, and passion fruit, freeze-dried yogurt is a tasty addition to your food storage.

Shelf-stable yogurt ingredients. Yogurt is easy to make and only requires a couple of ingredients: milk and yogurt starter. You can use existing yogurt as a starter or use a dry yogurt starter like Yogourmet freeze-dried yogurt starter or acidophilus tablets found in the vitamin section. (See the Make Your Own Yogurt sidebar.)

Cheese

Really, who wants to live without cheese? You don't have to have a cheese-less food storage with the many options for storing cheese.

Make Your Own Yogurt

1. Heat 1 quart (1L) of milk in a double boiler to 185°F (85°C). This high heat denatures the proteins in the milk and kills any foreign bacteria that may be present. If using powdered milk, mix 2 cups of powdered milk with 4 cups of water and blend well before heating.
2. Let the milk cool to approximately 110°F (43°C). The starter will not work reliably below 90°F (32°C) or above 120°F (49°C).
3. Add one of the following room temperature yogurt starters:
   - 2 tablespoons existing yogurt with live active cultures
   - 3 crushed acidophilus tablets
   - 1 packet commercial freeze-dried yogurt starter (follow the directions on the package)
4. Mix well, cover, and incubate for three to twelve hours for the yogurt to set. To incubate the yogurt, it needs to be kept warm, ideally between 100°F (38°C) and 115°F (46°C). Use one of these methods or devise your own:
   - yogurt maker
   - shelf-style dehydrator set at 115°F (46°C)
   - wrap in warm towels inside a picnic cooler
   - thermos or other insulated cooker
   - submerge containers partially in water inside a picnic cooler
   - a warm car window

   The longer the yogurt incubates, the more sour the taste will be.
5. When the yogurt has set, either drain the liquid (whey) or mix it in. For flavor variations, add jam, flavoring extracts, flavored gelatin, sweetener, or fruit.

Yogurt can be stored on the shelf for up to a week or in the refrigerator for two weeks. Be sure to save 2 tablespoons to start your next batch of yogurt!

Waxing cheese. Any mild hard cheese can be coated with cheese wax and stored on a shelf. Start with a mild cheese as it will age quickly. To wax cheese, melt cheese wax in a double boiler and either dip a block of cheese into the melted wax one half at a time or brush the wax on with a natural bristle brush. Paraffin wax can be used, but it is not as supple and tends to crack easily, exposing the cheese to air. Cheese waxes are thicker, more flexible, and keep light out as well. Unless you like super sharp cheese, waxed cheese should be used within three months for the best flavor.

Frozen cheese. Cheese will freeze for around three months. The texture does tend to lose its integrity after thawing, becoming crumbly and difficult to slice. For best results, allow the cheese to defrost completely before slicing or shredding.

Canned cheese. Shelf-stable canned cheese is available in the United States from online retailers. It is most often canned in Australia under the brand names of Red Feather, Bega, and Kraft. According to the manufacturers, it has an indefinite shelf life. This cheese is solid with a mild cheddar taste, although it will sharpen as it stores. Another variety of canned cheese, Cougar Cheese, available from the University of Washington in different flavor variations, has an indefinite shelf life if the can is kept refrigerated.

You can also purchase the #10 cans of nacho cheese sauce used by commercial kitchens. It is commonly available in warehouse stores and the bulk foods aisle of grocery stores. If this is too much cheese for one use, you can repackage and freeze whatever you want to save.

Cheese powders. Cheese powders mix up into a cheese sauce, a lot like the powder included in a box of macaroni and cheese. They are sold by most food storage retailers and add excellent cheese flavor to casseroles and soups.

Freeze-dried cheese. Mozzarella, cheddar, Colby, and Monterey Jack cheeses can all be stored as freeze-dried shredded cheese. Freeze-dried cheese has a shelf life of twenty-five years and even melts after it is reconstituted.

Make cheese. Many varieties of cheeses can be produced in your own home using fresh milk, milk from the store, or even powdered milk. From cottage cheese to cream cheese to cheddar, being able to make your own cheeses adds fresh cheese to your food storage plan. Making cheeses, especially the hard varieties, does require some specialized equipment and a little practice. To get started easily, pick up a beginning cheese-making kit from cheesemaking.com or homesteaderssupply.com. Both of those sites also carry cheese waxing supplies.

Butter

Frozen butter. Cubes of butter store well in the freezer for three to six months in their original packaging. Vacuum seal the butter either in the box or just in the paper wrapper for longer storage life. Frozen butter thaws nicely without any ill effects from being frozen.

Butter powder. Butter powder is available from most food storage suppliers. It mixes with water into a spread with excellent butter flavor. Powdered

Just Say NO to Canning Butter

Butter is one of the foods that should not be canned at home, even though instructions for canning butter abound online. Butter is a low-acid food with high fat content, and that fat can protect spores of bacteria like *C. botulinum* even at the high temperatures a pressure canner can achieve. It's not worth the safety risk to your family to can your own butter at home.

butter does not melt like fresh butter, so it should not be used as a substitute for fresh butter in baking.

Canned clarified butter. Clarified butter, also called ghee, is available canned in ethnic food stores. The World Grocer brand is carried by a few food storage companies. Make your own ghee by heating unsalted butter on very low heat for approximately forty-five minutes. Skim off any bubble scum that floats to the top, but don't stir the butter. The milk solids will collect at the bottom of the pan as it cooks. When it is done, pour the butter through a strainer, cheesecloth, or a coffee filter to catch the milk solids. The resulting filtered butter is the ghee. Ghee can be stored like any other oil at room temperature or in the refrigerator and will keep on the shelf up to two years.

Canned butter. Red Feather makes a commercially canned butter that is imported from New Zealand and is available online and from many preparedness retailers. The manufacturer claims an indefinite shelf life, and the butter behaves in cooking and baking like fresh butter. At around seven dollars for a 12-oz. can (equivalent to three sticks of butter), it's one of the more expensive butter storage options.

Make butter. If you have a dairy animal, you can use the cream to make butter with a butter churn or by agitating it in a jar either by shaking or rolling. In five to thirty minutes, the butter will thicken and separate from the buttermilk. Rinse it off to store it longer than a couple of days. Heavy cream powder is also available for purchase from some bakery supply stores and online. After reconstitution, this powder can be made into butter just like fresh cream.

Other Dairy Products

A few less common dairy products are also available in storage-friendly form, including buttermilk powder, sour cream powder, and heavy cream powder. Find them at food storage companies, restaurant supply stores, and online.

Dairy-Free Options

You can get milk in your food storage even with a dairy restriction. Shelf-stable soy, rice, or almond milks are perfect for short-term food storage. For long-term storage, try powdered soy milks available from Honeyville or other natural food retailers. Powdered rice milk is also available.

STORING FRUITS

Commercially canned fruit. Many fruits are readily available pre-canned at grocery stores. These canned fruits can store for three to five years if kept in a cool, dark, dry environment, making them perfect for short-term or mid-range storage.

Home-canned fruit. If you grow your own fruit or can get some at a farmers market or from a friend or neighbor, canning that fruit is a tasty and inexpensive way to preserve it. By canning your own fruit, you can have more variety than is available commercially, plus you have full control over the sugar content of the syrup. (See chapter five for instructions for canning fruit.)

Frozen fruit. Store-bought or home-picked fruits that are frozen will keep for eight to twelve months, making frozen fruit an acceptable storage solution for short-term food storage. Extend the shelf life by packaging your fruit with a vacuum sealer prior to freezing.

Dehydrated fruit. Fruits can be dehydrated at home or purchased commercially dehydrated. Raisins, apples, blueberries, apricots, and bananas are some of my favorites. Fruit leathers are also an excellent and delicious way to preserve fruit through drying. Properly stored, dehydrated fruits have a shelf life of up to twenty years.

Freeze-dried fruit. Pineapple, mangoes, strawberries, peaches, and oranges are among the many fruits that can be purchased freeze-dried. Freeze-dried fruits have a lighter texture than dehydrated fruits. They also have the longest shelf life of all methods of storing fruit—up to twenty-five years.

Grow your own fruit. Some small fruits like berries can provide fresh fruit annually within the first year or two after being planted. Other fruits, especially those that grow on bushes or trees, can take up to five years from the time they are planted to begin producing fruit. Check with your local extension agent for varieties of fruit that grow well in your area, and get some planted.

STORING VEGETABLES

Commercially canned vegetables. Potatoes, carrots, beans, peas, asparagus, and spinach are some of the vegetables available commercially canned at most grocery stores. These vegetables have approximately a three-year shelf life.

Home-canned vegetables. If you want to preserve a garden harvest or store specialized mixtures of vegetables, home canning is an excellent method of getting those vegetables into your food storage. By canning your own, you can also control the salt content. Remember that unless you are pickling your vegetables, they will need to be canned with a pressure canner. (See chapter five for instructions on canning vegetables.)

Frozen vegetables. Vegetables can be frozen for nine to twelve months and even longer if they are packaged with a vacuum sealer prior to freezing.

Dehydrated vegetables. Dehydrate your own fresh vegetables until brittle for longer-term storage. These vegetables are good eaten reconstituted as a side dish and are great in soups and stews. They have a shelf life of up to twenty years.

Freeze-dried vegetables. Freeze-dried vegetables have up to a twenty-five year shelf life and offer a wide variety of choices including corn, cauliflower, and asparagus. Unlike dehydrated vegetables that are very hard and therefore difficult to eat dry, freeze-dried vegetables have a light texture and can be eaten dry out of the can.

Grow your own vegetables. Most vegetable varieties are annuals, meaning they are planted and harvested in the same year. Keeping a fresh stock of garden seeds and knowing how to plant and grow them can provide vegetables for your food storage within a few weeks of planting.

STORING GRAINS

Grains provide the basis of many meals and provide the body with essential carbohydrates and energy. Grains are a large part of most long-term food storage plans because they store well and are easy to cook and eat. Hopefully, by this point, you can see that your food storage can be so much more than buckets of wheat. So here are some options for getting a variety of grains in your food storage.

Purchase canned. A wide variety of grains are available from most food storage suppliers already packed in #10 cans or buckets. Remember, you want a variety of grains including wheat, rice, oats, flours, dry corn, and pastas.

Purchase in bulk. Some suppliers offer grains in bulk. These will need to be repackaged for optimum shelf life, but a lot of times the money saved purchasing bulk grains is worth the time and supplies it takes to package it all.

Grow your own. This will require land and frequently some specialized equipment. You may not have the land or the equipment to grow your own grains, but occasionally you can partner with others who do to provide labor or pay in return for a portion of the harvest.

Whole vs. Processed Grains

All grains start out whole. They are then frequently ground into a coarse meal or fine flour or rolled or cut into flakes before reaching the store shelves. Rolled oats, pearled barley, white and wheat flour, rice flour, and cracked or flaked grains for hot cereals are all processed from their original form. These processed grains are easier to cook, requiring no special equipment like an oat roller or grain mill to be able to use them. However, grains store longest in their whole form like wheat berries or oat groats. Whole grains also give you options when you use them, like boiling whole, grinding into flour, sprouting, or rolling for cereal, as opposed to a processed grain, which is limited in the ways it can be used. So consider which form works best for you in your personal storage. If maximizing shelf life is your key consideration, invest in the tools to be able to use whole grains and store as much of your grains as possible in a whole form. If convenience is more important, store a variety of grains already processed so they're easy to use.

Gluten-Free Alternatives

Wheat is one of the most common grains consumed in the United States, and because of its long shelf life of thirty-plus years, it is also a favorite for long-term food storage. But what if you or someone in your family can't have wheat due to a gluten intolerance? Don't worry, there are a lot of other grains you can store. Here are some to get you started:

- quinoa
- millet
- buckwheat
- white or brown rice
- cornmeal
- oats (frequently contaminated with wheat during growing or processing, so make sure they are certified gluten-free before purchasing)
- sorghum
- amaranth
- popcorn

For those with extreme sensitivity to wheat products looking for long-term food storage, both Augason Farms and Thrive Life offer certified gluten-free products packed in #10 cans and buckets.

STORING OILS

When I first started storing food, I was told that the shelf life of oil was only about six months. I was concerned that any oil I had stored would go rancid before I could use it and storing oil would turn out to be a waste of money. This bit of advice actually had me choosing not to store oil at all. But it wasn't good advice. After much experimentation, I've found that oils can store much longer than a few months, and there is no reason not to have oil in your food storage.

Even with all the hype about reducing fat and oil in our food, healthy oils are an important part of our regular diets. They are used for cooking and baking, and stored properly can keep well for up to five years. Oils come in liquid forms like olive, canola, and vegetable oil, and solid like coconut oil, lard, and shortening.

For best results storing oils:

- Purchase a high-quality oil for storage. For liquid oil, olive oil is fantastic. It is also one of the more expensive oils, so you may need to purchase small amounts of it in addition to a less expensive vegetable oil. For solid oils, coconut oil and vegetable shortening both store well.
- Purchase oil in smaller containers. Older oil will go rancid faster after opening than fresh oil, so purchase your oil in containers that will be easy to use within a month or two after opening. I like the 48-oz. (1L) size bottles or smaller.
- Purchase oil in airtight containers. Lard has an especially short shelf life, primarily due to the non-airtight packaging it is sold in.
- Store your oil in a cool, dark place, out of high temperatures and away from light.

Good Oil Gone Bad

If oil in your storage has gone rancid and/or has an unappealing flavor or scent, all is not lost. You may not want to eat it, but that oil can still be used for a variety of purposes:

- Burn it in an oil lamp to provide some light.
- Pour some on your wood to help get a fire started.
- Oil leather products like horse tack and boots.
- Use it to make lye soaps.
- Oil tools like garden tools.

Make Personal Care Products With Oils

Oils like almond oil, coconut oil, and even lard can be used as moisturizers or to make lip balms or soap. Here's an easy lip balm recipe using some of our favorite oils.

Ingredients:

> By weight, measure into a double boiler:
>
> 20 percent beeswax
>
> 25 percent solid-at-room-temperature oil like coconut oil, palm oil, shea butter, or lanolin
>
> 15 percent brittle-at-room-temperature oil like cocoa butter or palm kernel oil
>
> 40 percent liquid-at-room-temperature oil like sweet almond oil, olive oil, or avocado oil
>
> Essential oil of your choice for scent—about ten drops per total ounce of lip balm (peppermint or orange are amazing, or make a mix for a custom scent)

Instructions:

Melt the oils and beeswax and pour the melted solution into small pots or lip balm tubes to cool. Enjoy your homemade all-natural lip balm!

STORING SEASONINGS

The same basic foods can become a variety of meals with a few seasoning changes.

Salt

Salt is a vital nutrient and stores indefinitely as long as it is kept away from moisture. Purchase salt in bulk or in boxes or shakers. For canning, you want canning or pickling salt that has not been iodized. Iodized salt is fine for seasoning foods. Some salts like Redmond Real Salt and some sea salts are not as heavily processed as table salts and include trace minerals in addition to the salt.

Herbs and Seasonings

Dried herbs. Little bottles of dried herbs will keep a good flavor for one to two years and are easy to find in the baking aisle of most grocery stores.

Freeze-dried herbs. Freeze-dried herbs have a flavor that is close to fresh herbs. They are not as common and usually are a little more expensive than dried herbs. Thrive Life sells seasonings and freeze-dried herbs packed in tiny cans with oxygen absorbers, giving them a twenty-five year shelf life.

Grow your own herbs. Herbs are easy to grow and make beautiful plants in either an outdoor garden area or in containers. Herbs like full sun and well-drained soil. Perennial herbs like sage, chives, thyme, and mint will return year after year. Annual herbs will need to be replanted each year and include basil, oregano, and cilantro. Some annuals like dill reseed themselves so easily they will probably show up in your garden again the next spring without being replanted. Let your dill go to seed and you'll likely have dill popping up in all sorts of unexpected places the following year.

STORING SWEETS

Not many of us want to survive without a little sweetener in our food storage. And it turns out that storing sweets is super easy.

Sugar

Granulated white sugar. This type of sugar has an indefinite storage life. It just needs to be kept away from moisture. Sugar can be purchased in packages of varying sizes from grocery stores and warehouse stores. Sugar is also available canned from food storage companies. If you transfer your sugar from the bags to another container, do not add oxygen absorbers! These will turn your nice sugar crystals into a big brick of sugar. Yes, you can still eat it, but not very easily.

Powdered sugar. Store powdered sugar away from moisture as well. Put the bag in a rodent-proof container. It does not need to be airtight. Powdered sugar also has an indefinite shelf life.

Make Brown Sugar

To always have soft brown sugar, make your own as you need it. Add 1 tablespoon of molasses to 1 cup of granulated sugar and mix with a fork until blended. By storing molasses and granulated sugar, you can have brown sugar in your long-term food storage!

Brown sugar. Brown sugar comes in varying grades. The more expensive brands like C&H stay soft longer than store brands. Brown sugar can be kept for up to a year and still be soft if it is stored in an airtight container. If your brown sugar hardens, warm it to soften it back up. As it cools it will reharden, so measure and use it while warm.

Honey

Keep your honey in a container with a tight-fitting lid. Honey will harden or crystallize over time, but can be re-softened by warming it slightly and stirring it. To make this softening easier, and to help eliminate some of the mess when you're using the honey, it is best to store it in containers no larger than 5 to 7 pounds (about ½ gallon).

Purchase honey from a store. Commercially processed honey has often been super filtered or treated at high temperatures to improve its appearance or keep it from crystallizing quickly. Check the label to be sure nothing else has been added to it.

Purchase from a beekeeper. Honey that has not been heat-processed or highly filtered, usually called raw honey, will have all the enzymes intact and is the healthiest for you. Buying from a beekeeper allows you to ask questions about their extraction process and purchase in bulk quantities. Sometimes the price is even better than at a grocer.

Keep your own beehives. Keeping honeybees is a fun and fascinating hobby. They do have some space requirements and you'll need some equipment to get started, but if you are successful at keeping hives of bees, you can have a continuous supply of raw local honey.

Other Sweeteners

Sweets don't end with honey and sugar. There is sugar in many other foods that can be stored as part of your food storage plan.

Jams and jellies. Store a few of these for spreading on sandwiches and flavoring baked goods. If you have access to fruit, the flavor of home-canned jams and jellies is definitely worth the work that goes into canning them.

Syrups. Corn syrup, maple syrup, and pancake syrup all have long shelf lives and add flavor and variety to your sweets. The syrups in canned fruit also contain sugar and can be used as a sweetener.

Molasses. Here's another sweetener with an indefinite shelf life. Molasses can also be used to make brown sugar from white sugar or dark corn syrup from light corn syrup.

Candy. Candies, including hard candies and chocolates, are best stored

Sweet Holidays

Baking sweets, including sugar, chocolate chips, and baking syrups, usually go on sale in late fall for Thanksgiving and Christmas baking. Those seasons are a great time to stock up on baking sweets.

Stores also sell seasonal candy for almost all holidays. After the holiday, these candies get marked down for quick sale, and you can pick some up less expensively for your food storage. It really won't matter when you want chocolate if it is wrapped in Valentine's Day packaging.

vacuum sealed in a jar to preserve freshness. Chocolate candies, including chocolate chips, can also be frozen. Stored on the shelf, they will last six to twelve months if you can keep from eating them. Freezing chocolate extends the shelf life to two to three years, and vacuum sealing it lengthens the shelf life to two to four years.

Drink mixes. Another source of sugar in your food storage is sweetened drink mixes. These can also help make treated water more palatable and are available in a variety of flavors. Some are even vitamin enhanced to add a few extra nutrients to your drink.

ORGANIC

A growing number of people want to eat and store organic foods. One of the easiest ways to do this is to can, dehydrate, or freeze foods grown in your own garden or obtained from an organic source. A few food storage companies also offer organic food lines. You can find organic food packed for long-term food storage from Survive 2 Thrive, Thrive Life, and PrepSOS.com.

SPROUTING

Did you know you can store fresh green food in your food storage? Even though fresh greens are a perishable item, you can grow your own fresh greens in a matter of days by storing sprouting seeds.

Why Sprout?

1. Sprouts are high in nutrition. It's like storing vitamins in your food storage. Before seeds sprout, they are dormant little plants. Sprouting changes the chemistry of the seed and adds vitamins and nutrients that weren't there before.

Sprouter Varieties

A sprouter is a container specifically designed to help seeds sprout. Sprouters come in a number of styles including the following.

Tray Sprouters

Tray sprouters work particularly well for long sprouts like alfalfa, fenugreek, radish, and clover as the tray configuration lets them grow up nice and straight. Grains and legumes also sprout nicely in tray sprouters. Look for a tray sprouter that you can do more than one batch in so you can have sprouts maturing at different times and don't have to wait for your first batch to finish (which can take up to a week) before starting a second batch. This can be accomplished with dividers or by having multiple trays or through a combination of both methods.

Jar Sprouters

Jar sprouters are as simple and inexpensive as they come. They consist of a jar like a mason jar and a

Tray, jar, and hemp bag sprouters

screened lid. There are companies that make mesh strainer lids and some that make a whole sprouting jar setup. Or just use a jar with some vinyl screen material from the hardware store over the opening. Hold the screening on with a rubber band or a metal canning ring. You can grow any kind of sprout in the jar, although the long sprouts aren't as pretty as when they are grown in a tray sprouter.

Hemp Bag Sprouters

Hemp bag sprouters work by keeping the sprouts moist inside a bag of wet hemp fabric. They are easy to use and extremely lightweight and portable. Smaller sprouts like alfalfa are a little tougher to get cleaned out of the bag, but anything can be sprouted in a hemp bag sprouter.

2. Sprouts grow fast and easily. You can have fresh produce in as little as three to five days, and it's so easy.

3. Sprouts require no soil and very little space to grow. You can grow fresh, nutritious foods with no garden plot. This is especially great if you live in a house with a small yard or in an apartment or rental house. You can even grow sprouts while you're traveling (think of the possibilities in an emergency kit)!

4. Sprouts grow during any season, and they don't require sunlight. You don't need to wait for spring or summer to plant and grow sprouts.

5. Mature sprouts are approximately two to ten times the volume of food as their dry seed counterparts. For example, 1 cup of wheat berries equals over 1¾ cups of sprouted wheat. Just ⅛ cup alfalfa grows to over 2 cups of sprouts! This means you can store a lot of food in a very small space.

So if you want a source for fresh food with some high nutritional content that is easy and quick to grow and adds variety and versatility to your food storage, you're going to love sprouting!

What to Sprout

To get started sprouting you'll need some sprouting seeds. Sprouting seeds come in two basic categories: vegetable seeds (like alfalfa, radish, clover, broccoli, and fenugreek) and legumes/grains (including chickpeas, mung beans, wheat, kamut, and lentils). In general, the vegetable varieties will take a little longer to grow because those are the ones you want to grow long and leaf out. The legumes/grains can be ready to eat within a couple of days as they are most often sprouted just until the "tail" starts to show. Occasionally the legumes and grains are sprouted longer, like bean sprouts for stir-fry or growing wheatgrass. You can also sprout some nuts like sunflower seeds, hazelnuts, and almonds.

You don't want to sprout tomato, potato, paprika, aubergine, eggplant, or rhubarb as they can be poisonous. Stick with a good supplier of sprouting seeds and this won't be an issue.

How to Sprout

Getting started sprouting is easy and enjoyable.
You will need:
sprouting seeds
bowl or jar
water
sprouter

1. Fill a jar or bowl with a volume of water that is three times the volume of the seeds you want to sprout (e.g., 3 cups of water for 1 cup of seeds). Soak your seeds in water six to eight hours. Some seeds soak up more than others, so make sure there is plenty of water covering your seeds.
2. Drain the soak water. Put the seeds in the sprouter.
3. Rinse and drain the seeds in the sprouter.
4. Put your sprouter in a dark place where you will not forget about it. I like to put mine in a kitchen cupboard that I frequently open for meals.
5. Rinse and drain the sprouts two to four times a day to keep them moist and clean. If you forget and the seeds dry out a bit, just get them nice and wet and let them try growing again. Usually they'll just pick up where they left off.
6. Allow the sprouts to grow to the desired length. Vegetable sprouts will usually take five to eight days, and legumes/grains can be ready to eat when they just have a tail sprouting—usually within twenty-four to forty-eight hours. Taste test the sprouts along the way and see at which stage you like them best.
7. To get your sprouts to turn green, allow them to sit in the sun once for four to six hours after the leaves have grown.
8. After the sprouts have reached the desired length, you can store them in the refrigerator for up to a week. Usually the sprouter makes an excellent crisper, so if you don't need it to start more seeds, you can store the sprouts in the sprouter they grew in.

SUMMARY

We really live in the golden age of food storage choices. With so many options for storing such a wide variety of foods, there is no reason to have boring "wheat and beans" food storage. You and your family will appreciate variety in your emergency meals—it's definitely better than eating only rice for every meal!

9. SUSTAINABLE FOOD STORAGE

Food stored in cans and buckets will eventually run out. Supplementing your stored food with sustainable food sources like gardening, livestock, or hunting will help extend the food supply you have as well as provide food for years to come. Plus it is one of the least expensive and healthiest ways to gather food for your family for everyday eating and storage.

GARDENING
It wasn't too many years ago that families kept gardens to produce much of their own food. Food was picked from the yard and cooked for dinner that night. Gardening gets us in touch with the land and can provide a wide variety of fruits, vegetables, and grains for consumption and storage at very little cost.

How Much Do You Need to Plant?
Even a small space can produce a lot of food. According to various sources, one-quarter acre of land planted densely with a variety of crops can produce an average of 2,660 pounds (1,207kg) of food per year. Your yield may be slightly less, depending on your planting layout, availability of water, soil type, and any disease or pest problems that can reduce garden production, but we're going to use the statistical number for simplicity. If that food is preserved to be used throughout the year, it can provide approximately 7 pounds (3kg) of food per day. For most foods, 1 pound (454g) will be approximately 2 cups of food, so it is possible to produce around 14 cups of food per day on a quarter acre. If this food will be the primary source of your stored food, remember to plant a

variety of crops so you're not eating 14 cups of tomatoes every day. Also have two plans for preserving that food, one in which you can use electricity and one to use if the power is out, like solar dehydrating or canning with a gas stove.

Ways to Maximize Planting Space

Not everybody has an area large enough to plant a quarter-acre garden. To make the best use of your available planting space, you may need to get creative.

Plant in beds. Plants do not need to be planted in rows. We plant in rows to make it easier for us to reach the plants to weed and harvest. To maximize your food-production space, plant in garden beds or wide rows. Make your garden beds just wide enough that you can reach the middle of them from one side or the other so you will be able to access your food. Now instead of two rows of beans in a 3-foot (91cm) width of garden, using the recommended spacing for bean rows, you can grow four rows next to each other, doubling your yield in the same amount of space.

Landscape with food. If your garden area is limited, plant vegetables and fruits in your landscaping in place of flowers or other ornamental plants. Most garden plants and especially herbs look nice as decorative plants. Need a ground cover? Plant strawberries. A hedge? Raspberries or grapes. With a little creativity, your landscape can be beautiful and feed you.

Plant in containers. For those severely limited in dirt space like renters or apartment dwellers, container gardening can give you fresh food even if you have no yard to use. Place your containers in full sun if possible, and water regularly since a plant's root system can only extend to the bottom of the container.

Seed Types

To start a garden, you'll need some seeds. For best results, start with fresh, quality seeds. When purchasing seeds, you'll find hybrid and non-hybrid (also called heirloom or open-pollinated) seeds. What's the difference?

Hybrid seeds. Without getting into a full genetics course, the crossing of two types of adult plants produces a hybrid seed. When these hybrid seeds are planted, they produce a new variation of that plant different from either of the parent plants. Hybrids have been developed to resist disease or to produce other traits like specific fruit size or shape. The trouble with hybrid seeds is that if that hybrid plant produces seed (which it may not—think seedless watermelon), there is no regularity in that seed. It might grow something like one of the parent plants, or it might grow something entirely different.

Sources for Heirloom Seeds

Need some non-hybrid seeds for your next garden? Try any of these fantastic resources:

- Baker Creek Heirloom Seed Company, **rareseeds.com**
- D. Landreth Seed Company, **landrethseeds.com**
- Seed Savers Exchange, **seedsavers.org**
- Sustainable Seed Company, **sustainableseedco.com**
- The Living Seed Company, **livingseedcompany.com**

Local living history farms or botanical gardens may also have heirloom seeds specifically suited to your area.

Non-hybrid seeds. Non-hybrid seeds produce plants that are exactly like their parent plants, and as long as the pollination process is not contaminated, they will continue to produce and grow the same plant for generations. Gardens can be planted with hybrid plants, but to be truly sustainable, harvesting and replanting seeds for future gardens, use non-hybrid seeds.

Survival seed banks. Many preparedness companies sell heirloom seed collections, commonly called seed banks or seed vaults, packaged for storage in a #10 can, Mylar bag, PVC tube, or other container. The premise is that you can store this can of seeds with your food storage, then pull it out and plant a beautiful garden in some future long-term disaster. The preselected variety of seeds takes the guesswork out of starting an heirloom garden, but it is not the solution for everyone. If the seed varieties are not well suited to your growing season or are varieties of vegetables you do not like or the price seems high for the seeds you are receiving, you will be better off purchasing seed packets à la carte from an heirloom seed company.

Either way you choose to get your seeds, do not just set them on a shelf and wait for a disaster. Seeds have a shelf life much shorter than most foods. A few will still grow ten years later, but many will no longer be viable, reducing your survival garden to just a few varieties of plants.

Gardening and saving seeds also comes with a learning curve. It is much better to plant those seeds now while you can buy food at the store or replenish

Tips for Saving Seeds

- Start with non-hybrid seeds. You want the seeds you save to grow the same plant next year.
- Some plants like carrots, beets, and onions are biennial, so they won't set seed until the second year. This means if you are planting them for survival, you'll need to split your initial seed supply to cover the first two seasons of planting while waiting for seeds to develop.
- A good seed-saving guide is invaluable. I use the book *Seed to Seed* by Suzanne Ashworth. Each plant has its own method for seed preservation, and knowing what needs to be done to preserve pure seeds will keep your future gardens producing the best food possible.

your seed stock if it turns out you have more of a brown thumb than a green one. The best way to grow a survival garden in some future disaster is to learn to grow a garden now.

Seed-Saving Techniques

Saving seeds from your own garden gives you the power to grow food again the following year without buying new seeds. It's not too hard, but techniques vary from plant to plant. We'll cover saving seeds from a few of the most common plants in this chapter.

Saving bean and pea seeds. Beans and peas are one of the easiest seeds to save. They are self-pollinating, so unless you purchased a variety that you know is a cross, the beans and peas you plant in your garden are almost certainly non-hybrid.

To save bean or pea seeds:

- Allow the pods to remain on the plant until they are dry.
- Pick them and remove the shells, saving the dry seeds.
- Seeds are dry and ready for storage when they break instead of smash when hit with a hammer.

Saving squash seeds. Squash plants will cross-pollinate easily, but only within their same species. Since there are four common species of squash, you can grow one variety in each species group and only chance cross-pollination if your neighbors are growing different varieties. Hand-pollination will also preserve pure seeds.

To save squash seeds:

- Allow the squash to grow to maturity on the vine. With summer squash, that means leaving them on the vine until they are large and the skin is hard.
- Cut the squash from the vine and allow it to sit for at least two to three weeks.
- Cut or break the squash open and remove the seeds.
- Rinse the seeds in a colander and lay them out to dry on a plastic or glass plate or cookie sheet.
- Seeds are dry and ready for storage when they break in half when bent.

Squash belong to the genus *Cucurbita* and one of six species. Four of those species—*C. maxima*, *C. mixta*, *C. moschata*, and *C. pepo*—contain the majority of common squash plants. Because squash do not cross-pollinate between species, choosing one from each species to plant will save you the trouble of hand-pollination to maintain a pure seed line.

C. maxima species of squash include: banana, buttercup, Hubbard, sweetmeat, and turban.

C. mixta species of squash include: cushaw (except golden cushaw, orange cushaw, and orange striped cushaw), seroria, and silver seed gourds.

Hand Pollinating

Plants in the squash and cucumber families can be easily hand pollinated to save pure seeds for replanting or to aid in the pollination rate of the plant.

1. Identify the male and female blossoms. Male flowers are usually on a short, thin stem and sometimes grow in clusters. Female flowers have a small immature fruit where the flower connects to the plant.
2. On the day the female flower opens, use a soft paintbrush or cotton swab to brush the inside of the male flower, collecting pollen.
3. Carefully brush the inside of the female flower with the brush to distribute the pollen.
4. If you are planning to save seeds from the fruit, gently close the female flower back up after pollination and secure loosely with tape to keep out pollinating insects. Mark the fruit by loosely tying a ribbon around the stem of the fruit so you will remember which one to save for seeds.

Garden Perennials

Most garden plants like peppers and tomatoes need to be planted each year, but many food plants are perennial, meaning they come back on their own year after year, saving you the work of replanting each year. Most fruits, some herbs, and even a few vegetables are perennials. Plant them once and they grow for years. Not all will grow in every climate, so check with your local extension office if you have any questions about what will grow in your area. Here are some of the more common garden perennials.

Vegetables: asparagus, Jerusalem artichoke, rhubarb

Herbs: chives, fennel, garlic, ginger, horseradish, mint, oregano, rosemary, sage, thyme

Fruits: blackberries, currants, figs, huckleberries, grapes, raspberries, strawberries

Tree fruits: apples, apricots, cherries, nectarines, oranges, peaches, pears, plums

C. moschata species of squash include: butternut, cheese, and golden, orange, and orange striped cushaw.

C. pepo species of squash include: acorn, crookneck, pumpkin, zucchini, and small decorative, striped or warty gourds.

Saving cucumber seeds. Cucumbers will readily cross with each other, so hand-pollination is best to preserve pure seed. Seeds of cucumber are contained in a gelatinous sack similar to tomato seeds.

To save cucumber seeds:

- Allow the cucumber to get large and soft on the vine. This will be past the normal time you would harvest for eating.
- Cut the cucumber from the vine and let it sit protected from direct sun for two weeks to allow the seeds to mature.
- Carefully cut open the cucumber and scoop the seeds into a bowl.
- Add as much water as seeds and allow to ferment for two to three days.
- Seeds will sink to the bottom as they separate from the gel sacks. Strain and wash the seeds.
- Lay the seeds out to dry on a glass or hard plastic plate or cookie sheet.
- Fully dry seeds snap instead of flexing when bent.

Saving tomato seeds. Tomatoes are delicious and versatile and can be used in a variety of meals and sauces. Due to the design of their flower, tomatoes do not cross-pollinate readily, so seeds saved from an heirloom tomato will grow the same tomato when planted the following year.

To save tomato seeds:

- Pick and wash fully ripe tomatoes.
- Cut tomatoes through the middle to expose the seeds.
- Squeeze the seeds and surrounding gel into a bowl. Small tomatoes can be mixed into a paste in a blender at low speed without damaging the seeds.
- Add as much water as tomato and allow the mixture to sit and ferment for two to three days. Mold may form on the surface and it won't smell good, so keep it where it won't get spilled!
- Once the seeds have sunk to the bottom and separated from the gel, strain and wash the seeds.
- Lay the seeds out to dry on a glass or hard plastic plate or cookie sheet.
- Seeds are dry and ready for storage when they easily slide across the plate and don't clump together.

Herb Gardening

When my younger sister got married, she gave little potted herb plants as a wedding favor. I took home sage and chives, put them in the ground, and that was the humble start of my herb garden. Growing your own herbs is a tasty way to get a lot of flavor variety in your meals, whether you are eating food storage or not. You can also plant medicinal herbs in your herb garden. Herbs are super easy to grow and look nice enough to have in your front yard. Most grow best in full sun and well-drained soil. Here are a few of my favorites:

Culinary: basil, chives, dill, mint, oregano, parsley, sage

Medicinal: blue hyssop, chamomile, echinacea (purple coneflower), feverfew, horehound, lemon balm

Practice Makes Perfect

Gardening takes practice, especially if you live in a location where the conditions of the soil, sun, and water are not perfectly aligned for the plants you are trying to grow, which is almost everywhere. There will be good years and not-so-good years. Some plants will thrive and others will dive.

Consult with other local gardeners or your local county extension office for help with gardening in your specific area. (Find your local office at **www. csrees.usda.gov/Extension**.) Starting a garden, even if it is only with a few plants, will provide your family with a renewable source of tasty and healthy homegrown foods.

KEEPING ANIMALS

Fresh meat, eggs, milk, and honey can all be added regularly to your food stores by raising animals. Some animals can be kept in small yards, and others need larger areas. Following are some common food-providing animals and the basic requirements for each. If you find one that will work for you, consult with local experts, your county extension office, and reputable guidebooks for more information and to answer any questions you may have about keeping that animal.

SMALL ANIMALS

Chickens

Raising backyard chickens has grown in popularity over the last few years, and for good reason. These little birds can provide meat, eggs, and company and don't require a lot of space or maintenance. Check your local regulations regarding backyard chickens and you might be able to get a few egg layers even on a small lot in town.

Meat breeds. Chicken breeds that are good for meat production are Cornish Cross, Jersey Giant, and Delaware. Meat birds are ready to hit your freezer or canner when they are between six and ten weeks old. Each bird will provide approximately 5 pounds (2kg) of meat.

Laying breeds. Chicken breeds that are good for egg production are Australorp, Black or Brown Sex Link, Orpington, Plymouth Rock, Rhode Island Red and Ameraucana. Three hens will give you approximately two eggs every day through the spring, summer, and fall. In most climates, hens do not lay through the winter months as a natural response to the decreased amount of daylight. Providing the hens with at least fourteen hours of light per day (by adding an electric light to the coop) can keep hens laying year round.

What Chickens Need

- A safe place to roam with approximately 10 square feet (1 square meter) per bird. Fences should be high enough that the chickens can't get out and predators can't get in. If you are going to free range, be sure it is not in an area with known chicken predators like foxes or roaming dogs, or among plants you don't want eaten.
- An enclosed coop with approximately 4 square feet (⅓ square meter) of floor space per bird and raised areas to roost.
- Laying boxes in the coop for eggs.
- Constant supply of fresh water and food. Chickens eat corn-based feed, bugs, plants, and most kitchen and garden scraps. Supplement with oyster shell or crushed egg shells for calcium.

- If you are planning to breed and hatch new chicks, you'll need at least one rooster and either a hen that will set on the fertilized eggs or an incubator.

Rabbits

Rabbits provide the most meat for the least amount of feed of any livestock animal. They are quiet and require very little time and space. They can be kept indoors in a barn or even in your house. Rabbits do not qualify as livestock, so it is unlikely your town or neighborhood will have restrictions on owning them.

Meat breeds. The best meat breeds of rabbits are the New Zealand, Californian, and Beveren. A doe can have from six to ten kits per litter, depending on the breed, and they are ready to butcher in eight to ten weeks. Each rabbit will provide about 3 pounds (1kg) of meat.

The doe can be bred again after the kits are weaned, which is around six weeks after birth. With a gestation period of twenty-eight to thirty-one days, one doe can provide around 24 pounds (11kg) of meat every 2½ months.

As an added value, you can save and tan the skins into thin leather that can be sewn into clothing items or crafts.

What Rabbits Need

- A predator-proof cage or hutch at least five times larger than the animal itself. If the rabbit is living outdoors, a portion of that cage should be an enclosed living area to keep warm and escape the weather.
- Bedding material in the enclosed area of the hutch.
- Shade. Rabbits are wearing a fur coat year round and can die from exposure to too much heat.
- Free access to food and water. Water should be dispensed from a water bottle to keep it clean and contained. Rabbits can be fed rabbit pellets, hay, and other garden and yard produce like grass clippings and vegetables.
- To breed rabbits, you'll want at least one female (doe) and one male (buck) in separate cages. You'll also need a separate area to remove the young to after weaning.

Bees

Honeybees are generally peaceful animals kept for the sole purpose of providing honey. There is a fairly substantial up-front investment in equipment for owning bees, but they do not need a lot of space and can be kept in a backyard. While your neighbors may not even notice your hives, it is a good idea to let them know you will be keeping bees, and don't set your hives next to a fence with small children or a neighbor with bee allergies on the opposite side. Join a local beekeeping organization, or network with other beekeepers in your area for help. A good reference book like *Beekeeping For Dummies* will also help you get started on the right foot.

The best breeds for honey production are Italian and Carnolian. Each hive of bees can provide between 4 to 6 gallons (15 to 23L) of honey (which is 48 to 72 pounds, 22 to 33kg) per year. Wax can also be harvested from the comb for making candles or adding to personal care items like lip balm, soaps, and moisturizing bars.

What Bees Need
- A hive body box with frames to build comb on. Most hives need at least two hive body boxes to provide for their own upkeep. The hive should include a bottom board and inner and outer lids. Keep the hive off the ground in a location with at least partial shade.
- Queen excluder grate applied to the top of the hive bodies before adding the honey supers. This grate keeps the egg laying to the hive body boxes, making the bees use the honey super boxes strictly for honey.
- Honey supers—shorter boxes with frames for building comb and storing honey. These are stacked on top of your queen excluder one at a time as needed.
- A nearby fresh water source.
- To access the hives, you will need some additional equipment for yourself including a smoker, bee suit with veil, hive tool, and bee brush.
- To extract honey, you'll need some form of extractor. These can be shared between beekeepers to cut down on costs, or some beekeepers will allow you the use of their extraction equipment for a small fee or a portion of your honey.

LARGE ANIMALS
Goats
My family kept up to four goats at a time on a quarter-acre lot that also housed our home, yard, and garden. Goats do not require a large amount of space. They are fairly low maintenance, but contrary to popular stereotypes will not eat just anything, including many weed varieties. Goats are generally considered an agricultural animal, so be sure your property is zoned to allow them.

Meat breeds: The best breeds of goat for meat production are Boer, Fainting Goat, and Kinder. Most does will have one or two kids per pregnancy,

although they can occasionally have up to four. Young goats are ready to butcher between six and eight months old and depending on the breed can provide up to 50 pounds of meat each.

Dairy breeds: The best breeds of goat for milk production are Alpine, LaMancha, Nubian, Saanen, and Toggenburg. A dairy goat doe will produce about 3 quarts (3L) of milk a day for ten months after birthing. To continue to produce milk, she will need to be bred each year and milked twice daily. Goat milk can be used for drinking or making other dairy products like cheese and yogurt.

A dairy goat doe can be bred with a meat goat buck to produce offspring that are genetically better for weight gain and butchering than a straight dairy goat. Do not breed a small doe with a large breed buck as it could cause complications with birthing.

What Goats Need

- Well-fenced living area with a minimum of 25 square feet (2 square meters) per animal.
- Shelter from the elements. A barn or three-sided structure with a minimum size of 15 square feet (1 square meter) per animal.
- Year-round supply of feed high in roughage like hay, brush, field grass including weeds, and grain. Goats are browsers, not grazers, so they do not thrive in a grass field, but prefer brush and hay.

- Fresh water.
- Salt and mineral lick blocks.
- If keeping a male for breeding, he'll need separate living quarters from the females.

Sheep

Requirements for sheep are similar to goats. They are not good milk producers, and are kept primarily for meat and wool. The best breeds of sheep for meat and wool are Dorset, Hampshire, Rambouillet, and Suffolk.

Ewes are bred in the fall and lamb in the spring, usually producing two lambs, but occasionally one or three lambs are born. Lambs are ready for butchering between eight and twelve months old. The average 90-pound (41kg) lamb will provide approximately 40 pounds (18kg) of meat. Sheep can also be sheared for wool, usually once a year in the spring.

What Sheep Need
- Well-fenced living area with a minimum of 25 square feet (2 square meters) per animal.
- Shelter from the elements. A barn or three-sided structure with a minimum size of 12 square feet (1 square meter) per animal.
- Year-round supply of feed high in roughage like hay, brush, field grass including weeds, and grain.
- Fresh water.
- Salt and mineral lick blocks.
- If keeping a male for breeding, he'll need separate living quarters from the females.

Pigs

With their large litters and quick growing rate, pigs can provide your family with plenty of pork chops, bacon, and ham. The best breeds of pig for meat production are Berkshire, Blue Butt, Hampshire, Large Black, and Yorkshire. Or purchase your pigs from a local breeder for a variety that works well in your area.

Pigs can have litters up to twice a year, averaging ten to twelve piglets per litter. Pigs are ready for butchering at about six months of age and provide approximately 140 pounds (64kg) of meat per 200-pound (91kg) pig.

What Pigs Need
- Sturdy fencing, especially low on the fence to discourage digging. Pigs need about 12 square feet (1 square meter) per animal in the yard. They can also be pastured in larger well-fenced areas.

Meat-Processing Options

Whether you raise livestock or hunt wild game, the animal will need to be processed for the meat. You have a couple of options to get this done.

1. Use a meat-processing facility. You can take your live agricultural animal or freshly harvested wild animal to a local meat-processing facility for processing. Some will even arrange to pick up your large animals at your location. The facility will dispatch the animal if it is delivered alive, and then cut, process, and wrap the meat from your animal for you. To find a reputable processing facility, ask others in your area who hunt or raise meat animals for a recommendation, or search online using the keywords "butchering" or "meat processing" and the name of your town. Most of these facilities do not process small animals like chickens or rabbits.

2. Process the meat yourself. This is more time-consuming, but you also have complete control over the cuts of meat you package. If you want to get started processing your own meat, I recommend *The Complete Book of Butchering, Smoking, Curing, and Sausage Making: How to Harvest Your Livestock & Wild Game* by Philip Hasheider, an excellent reference on butchering and processing animals both wild and domestic.

- Barn or other enclosure for shade and shelter.
- Feed. Corn-based pig feed is available at most farm and ranch stores as Starter, Grower, and Finisher. Using each of these at the appropriate time will help you get the most meat from your pig. Pigs can also be fed garden and orchard scraps.
- Lots of fresh water. Each pig will drink 1 to 2 gallons (4 to 8L) per day. Feeders and water dispensers should be securely anchored to the side of the pen to prevent the pigs from rooting underneath and spilling it.
- If breeding, separate living quarters is required for the male pig.

Cows

If you have the space for cows, they can be an excellent source of fresh milk and meat. Cows are one of the largest domestic meat animals, so they do have space requirements above the other animals we have discussed. They also provide the largest amount of meat at butchering time, which will need to be stored in a freezer or bottled for future use.

Breeds to Look For

- Dexter are smaller cows that produce 1½ to 2 gallons (6 to 7L) of milk per day.
- Jersey are midsized cows producing around 6 gallons (23L) per day.
- Holstein or Guernsey have a high milk production at around 12 gallons (45L) per day.

Cows bred once a year can produce milk ten months of the year. Cows need to be milked twice daily while lactating and provide between 1½ and 12 gallons (6 to 45L) of milk per day, depending on the breed. Calves are ready for slaughter at around two years of age. Each 1,000 pound (454kg) cow will provide approximately 500 pounds (227kg) of meat.

What Cows Need

- Between ½ and 2 acres of fenced pasture per cow.
- Shelter for protection in the winter and a place to milk comfortably.
- Hay and grain for additional feed, especially in areas with harsh winters.
- Plenty of clean water.
- Salt and mineral blocks.

STORING AND GROWING FEED FOR LIVESTOCK

You are keeping animals to provide yourself and your family with healthy meat, eggs, and milk. In order for the animal to provide food for you, you will need to provide food for it. If you have animals, consider their needs in your food storage plan and keep a supply of feed on hand for them. Most livestock can have their feed supplemented with garden scraps and excess produce, or you can use a portion of your garden to grow feed especially for the animals like barley grass, feed corn, or mangel beets. When animals are part of your food storage plan, your food storage plan needs to include feed for the animals.

WILD FOOD

Hunting, trapping, and foraging for food dates back to the earliest humans and is still a viable source of food for your family today.

Hunting

From duck to squirrel to deer, wild game provides a lean, healthy source of meat. The ability to hunt for food gives you an alternate means of getting meat protein into your food storage plan. Costs involved include license fees, weapons and ammunition, and travel expenses if your hunting location is not local.

Before heading into the hills to harvest a deer, here are the steps you'll need to take to get started.

1. Check with your state wildlife agency for regulations on the animals you want to hunt.
2. Pass a Hunter's Safety or Hunter's Education Course. These courses are available in all states and only need to be taken once. The curriculum should cover all the basics you'll need to know, including hunting and firearm safety, ethics, and shot placement.
3. Practice shooting your weapon. If you don't own a firearm, ask for help learning what you need from a friend, firearm dealer, or local gun range. Most gun owners are happy to help someone else learn to shoot responsibly.
4. Buy a license. Licenses are specific to game species and geographical area.
5. Familiarize yourself with the animal and area you are hunting. Learn their behavior, habits, routines, and probable locations prior to the hunt. Also learn how to take care of the meat after the animal is harvested.
6. Review firearm safety and notify a buddy where you're going before heading out to enjoy your hunt.

Selecting the right gun for your game. Game is best hunted with a bullet size that will be large enough to kill the animal quickly, but not so large that it damages too much meat. Caliber measures the diameter of the bullet a rifle will shoot either in inches or millimeters. The smaller the number, the smaller

GAME	SHOTGUN GAUGE
Small birds: Quail, chukar	20
Medium birds: Grouse, pheasant, duck	12, 20
Rabbit	12, 20

GAME	RIFLE CALIBER
Small game: rabbit, squirrel	.22LR, .17HMR
Midsize game: deer, antelope	.243 Win., .270 Win., .308 Win., .30-06 Spfd., .30-30 Win.
Large game: Elk, moose	.270 Win., 7x64, .308 Win., .30-06 Spfd., .338 Federal, .405 Win., .450 Marlin

the diameter of the bullet. Shotguns are measured by gauge, which is determined by the number of lead balls of a designated diameter it would take to make one pound of that size lead ball. Shotgun gauge numbers get larger as the diameter of the ball gets smaller. The preceding charts give common calibers and gauges for different game and are in no way an exhaustive list of firearms that could be used for each game species.

Practice. Just going hunting does not guarantee you'll bring home meat, and there is a definite learning curve to doing it well. Getting well practiced with your weapon of choice and hunting techniques will help raise your odds of having a successful hunt. Once an animal is harvested, the meat needs to be processed properly and thoroughly cooked to avoid effects from parasites and any possible disease in the animal. Learning to process game meat yourself can save the cost of taking it to a packaging facility.

Hunting is an excellent way to acquire naturally fed game meat for your family and food storage. However, do not rely on hunting as a primary means of feeding your family in a large-scale or long-term disaster. Currently, state wildlife agencies manage herds for specific population sizes through the limiting of available permits and use of specific hunting seasons. If everyone decides to take to the hills and hunt to survive, those populations will decrease rapidly and may become unsustainable. It is far more secure to have food stored than to depend on your hunting ability and the availability of wild game in a long-term disaster.

Trapping

Trapping is currently primarily used to capture fur-bearing animals. Trapping animals such as beaver, muskrat, raccoon, and nutria can also provide meat for your family or your pets. The pelts of fur bearers can be sold for extra income or tanned and used for clothing or crafts. Having the ability to trap wild animals could be a highly useful skill in a long-term disaster, keeping nuisance animals at bay and providing meat from sources not normally in high demand.

To get started trapping, contact your state wildlife agency for rules and license requirements for trapping in your area. Acquire approved trapping equipment and/or practice building primitive traps that could trap animals common where you live.

Fishing

Fishing can provide food for your family from nearby bodies of water. Besides catching food, fishing is an enjoyable hobby for most who participate in it.

Fishing First Steps

- Decide where you want to fish. Make sure it is a body of water with fish in it and that it is legal to fish there.
- Check with your state wildlife agency for information about licenses and the regulations for the water you will be fishing. States with both fresh and salt water may have two different licenses.
- Learn about the fish. Know what they like to eat, how large they are, what you need to catch them, and how to clean and cook one once you've caught it. Talk to other anglers or find fishing reports in your local newspaper or on your state wildlife agency's website.
- Let a friend know where you're going, or better yet, take one with you when heading out on your fishing adventure. Take your family members and teach them to fish.

Fishing equipment. Fishing gear will vary depending on the type and size of fish you are planning to catch as well as the water you will be fishing in, but here are some basic freshwater fishing necessities:

- A fishing pole. Most poles have a reel on them, but it is possible to fish without a reel.
- Fishing line. For small fish like panfish or trout, 4- to 6-pound line is fine. Larger fish will need heavier line.
- Hooks. The hook needs to fit in the fish's mouth, but too small of a hook may not catch a larger fish. An assortment of hook sizes will ensure you have the size you need.
- Sinkers. Weights help keep your bait low in the water where the fish can find it.
- Bobbers. Sometimes called floats, bobbers are used to hold bait off the bottom of the lake and give a visual signal when a fish takes the hook.
- Lures. You'll want an assortment of lures in styles that work well for the fish you are trying to catch.
- Bait. Live bait like worms or grasshoppers can be caught locally or purchased prior to the fishing trip. Other baits available include salmon eggs, marshmallow and moldable dough baits, plastic worms, and jigs.
- Insect repellent. This isn't to catch fish, but fishing requires you to be near water where there tend to be more insects. Insect repellent will keep you from having to leave early to avoid the bugs!

Fishing may not be a sustainable food-producing option for your family in a long-term disaster. Many inland fishing areas are stocked regularly by state wildlife agencies for anglers to fish. Popular fishing lakes and streams could quickly become depleted if they are not able to be replenished with these fresh populations of fish. Having a supply of food put away and supplementing that supply with fresh caught fish is a better plan than relying on fish as the primary source of your food.

WILD EDIBLE PLANTS

Mother Nature has provided us with many plants for our benefit and use. Knowing wild edible plants in your area can add to your regular diet as well as provide a food source in an emergency. Before you go out foraging and eat whatever green thing is growing in your yard, it's important to go over a couple of basic rules for eating from the wild.

1. Positive identification. You need to be able to properly identify the plant every time you find it. Know if there are look-alikes that are not safe to eat and how to avoid them. If you are not 100 percent sure the plant is safe to eat, move on to something else. I like to stick to plants that are common and easy to identify.
2. Do not eat any plants growing in questionable locations (e.g., areas sprayed for weeds). Stick to places you know are safe to eat from.
3. Use a field guide, or better yet a person with experience with wild edibles, to help you find and identify edible plants near you. One helpful field guide is *A Field Guide to Edible Wild Plants* by Lee Allen Peterson.

There are hundreds of wild edible plants. Here are a few of my favorites that can be found in most areas of the United States.

Dandelion

The lovely yellow flower most people try desperately to remove from their yards while children are happily blowing the seeds from here to the ends of the earth is edible from top to bottom. Dandelions have jagged dark green leaves and yellow flowers that turn to balls of fluff when they are ready to seed. They are one of the first plants to grow in a barren area and can be found in almost all climates of the world.

How to eat dandelion. The entire dandelion plant can be used for food. Eat the leaves raw in salad or steamed like spinach. Use the blooms for tea or jelly, eat them raw, or batter and fry them. Roots can be eaten boiled or roasted. Remove the outermost layer prior to eating by peeling with a knife or boiling them and slipping the outer layer off similar to a beet.

Purslane

Purslane, officially named *Portulaca oleracea*, can grow anywhere there is at least a two-month growing season, making it one of the most common "weeds"

Dandelion

Purslane

Prickly pear cactus

in the world. It is a low-growing succulent with thick red stems and smooth, flat, paddle-shaped leaves. In some countries purslane is specifically cultivated for eating. High in vitamin E and beta carotene, purslane is also an excellent source of essential omega-3 fatty acids.

How to eat purslane. Eat every part of purslane but the root. The leaves, stems, and flowers can be eaten raw and are good in salads or on sandwiches. Cook them like spinach or use them in a soup or stir-fry. Purslane has a slight lemony taste and also can be pickled or blended in a green smoothie.

Prickly Pear Cactus

You don't have to live in the southwest United States to find a prickly pear cactus. These cactus range from Alaska to South America and can be found in wet and dry climates. The prickly pears include around two hundred species of cacti under the genus name *Opuntia*. They typically grow in flat, paddle-shaped segments with large spines as well as small, hair-like spines on the pads and pear-shaped fruit.

How to eat prickly pear cactus: Use caution when working with cactus. Pliers and gloves might help keep you from getting pricked. Remove the spines from the fruit and pads by rubbing them with a coarse grit, burning them off, or cutting the outer layer including the spines away from the inner succulent section. Seeds of the fruits are edible, but are very hard and should be removed. Slice the pads and use them as vegetables. Cooking lessens the gelatinous mouth feel.

Wild Berries

You've probably been told not to eat any wild berries, and indeed some can make you very sick. But many will not. This is where we come back to rule number one about being able to positively identify your wild edible plant 100 percent of the time. Blackberries, raspberries, huckleberries, strawberries, currants, and elderberries are among the edible berries that can be found growing wild. Choose one or two that grow near you and become an expert at identifying those plants. Most are very similar in look to their domestically cultivated varieties, but be sure to use a good field guide or learn from someone else who is experienced in identifying wild berries in your region.

How to eat wild berries: Most edible berries growing in the wild are excellent eaten fresh from the plant. They can also be used as you would use cultivated berries in desserts and pastries. The more tart varieties like elderberry and currant are excellent for jellies or jams. Unripe elderberries are poisonous, so if you are using them, they must be picked fully ripe and are best cooked prior to eating.

SUMMARY

Food for your family does not all have to come from a store. With a little help from Mother Nature, you can provide a great deal of your own food through sustainable means. Growing a garden, raising livestock, and gathering food from the wild through hunting and foraging are sources of inexpensive, nutritious food for everyday eating and storage.

10. ORGANIZING AND STORING YOUR FOOD STORAGE

As you build your food storage, you'll acquire quite a collection of cans, buckets, and bottles and they all have to go somewhere until you're ready to use them. Finding space for it all is one of the biggest challenges of having food storage. But it is a challenge that can be conquered with a little creativity and organization.

COMBAT THE ENEMIES OF FOOD STORAGE

Remember the seven enemies of food storage—temperature, light, oxygen, moisture, pests, handling, and time. We covered some ways to battle these problems through proper packaging, but with a little planning, your storage areas can be a defense against them as well.

Temperature

Finding a storage area with a year-round cool temperature is ideal. Temperature is the primary reason basements and cellars are one of the best places for storing food. High temperatures, as well as wide fluctuations in temperature, will shorten the shelf life of your stored foods. Close or block heat vents in the room your food is stored in to help keep the temperature down.

Light

Block windows in your food storage areas if possible to keep sunlight out. Windows are a source of light and heat, so blocking them will do double duty to help keep your food fresh.

Oxygen

This really needs to be solved with your packaging. There's no real way to limit oxygen in a storage area unless you have an airtight vault in your home you can flush oxygen out of. You don't? Me neither. Just pack your food properly to minimize the effects of oxygen on it.

Moisture

Be sure your food storage area does not have the danger of getting wet. Raise food off the floor using pallets or boards to protect it from flooding and to prevent the condensation that can occur when a can of food is in direct contact with a hard floor like concrete.

Pests

While it may be impossible to keep them all out, a regular patrol of your food storage for signs of pests like rodents or insects can help nip the problem in the bud. Use a deterrent of your choice like mousetraps or sticky traps that catch bugs and mice to help protect your food, and always seal your containers after opening them.

Handling

Once your food is placed, the less it is moved around, the better off it will be. Some containers are better suited to being moved and experiencing rough handling than others, but all of them can sustain damage with repeated moving around. Ideally, you want your food storage easily accessible so you are not constantly shuffling cans and boxes around to get what you need. With most storage systems, it helps to store loose cans and jars in boxes. Boxes give support and structure to your cans and jars; plus a box makes it easier to move and stack them when needed.

Less Than Ideal Beats Not At All

So you don't have a room that is cool, dark, dry, and full of rotation shelving for your food storage? That's okay. If your storage area is less than ideal, store food in it anyway. To combat the shortened shelf life of a warm or humid environment, just eat that food sooner. As my husband once said, "I'd rather have a stack of food storage in the middle of my living room than not be able to feed my family."

Time

The best defense against the effects of time on your food storage is rotation. Keep the foods you have stored rotating into your regular meals, and use the oldest items first. A storage area designed to help rotate your food is an excellent way to avoid having mystery food in the dark recesses of your food storage room getting old and unusable. The Shelving Options section of this chapter will help you design such a storage area.

STORAGE LOCATIONS

Even if you are living in a small space like an apartment, condo, or trailer, you can find places to store some food. Don't let a perceived lack of space keep you from acquiring the food you need to feed your family. Let's take a walk through your house and explore some places that you may be able to store your food. After you've considered all your options, use the Food Storage Location worksheet in the appendix (or download a copy at **www.livingreadyonline.com/ foodstorage**) to help you prepare and stock food storage areas in your home.

Basement or Cellar

If you have a basement or cellar in your home, you have an excellent place to store food. Find a room or corner that is away from basement windows and block heat vents to that area. Even a crawl space under a house can be used for food storage if the moisture can be mitigated. Lay down boards or another ground covering so your food isn't sitting directly on the dirt. A little moisture is actually a benefit if you are storing raw root crops like potatoes and carrots.

Living Room

Yes, you can store food in your living room without piling it in the middle of the room. Pull a couch away from the wall and you can fit water bottles, buckets, or cases of cans stacked on their sides. If you're really crafty, you can build a custom rotation rack (see the Shelving Options section in this chapter) to fit behind your couch, then load cans in one side and pull from the other side. With #10 cans, you're only losing about 8 inches (20cm) of floor space by moving your couch away from the wall.

Some couches are on legs and can hide short items like cases of tuna under them. Coffee tables and end tables are candidates for hiding food storage as well. If you don't have a lot of furniture, you can make a coffee table or end table out of your food. Use cases of cans or buckets as a base, and lay a board or piece of plexiglass on top of them. Cover it all with a tablecloth and no one's the wiser.

Boxes stored behind a couch

Rolling shelf made to fit the space between a refrigerator and wall

Pull-down attic access ladder

Bedrooms

Convert a spare bedroom into a food storage room. Or just take over a closet. If you don't have a room or closet to spare, you may still be able to stack food in the back or on the bottom of closets, or build a nightstand like the coffee table example above.

Under and around beds is another area that can store a lot of food. The average twin bed can store at least forty-eight #10 cans under it. If you can access both sides of the bed, loading in one side and pulling from the opposite side will help with food rotation. For storing items larger than soup cans, your beds may need to be propped up with risers to accommodate the height of the food. With smaller items like canned fruits and soups, use rolling under-bed storage bins for easy accessibility.

Pull the bed away from the wall and stack food behind the headboard. Just like the couch, you're not losing much space in your room by doing this, and a lot of food can be stored out of sight in that space if it's stacked well.

Bathrooms

I would not recommend storing food in a bathroom that gets used frequently. There will be heat and moisture issues from steam condensation. Bathrooms are great for storing paper products like tissues or extra toilet paper, though. If you have a spare bathroom that rarely gets used (with four children it's hard to believe this is even possible), by all means use the cupboards, under the sink, or even fill the bathtub with food storage.

Kitchen

You already have food in the pantry and in cupboards, and it might take just a little bit of reorganizing to be able to fit a few more cans in. That empty space above the cupboards is great as well. Hide your food there in plain sight with some decorative bins or crates. And what about those high or deep shelves that are the abyss of all the kitchen utensils and plates you never use? Clear some of those out and you can put food there. With deep cupboards, line the back edge with cans of food and you'll still have room to stack plates and cups in front of them.

Some kitchens have a nice slot of wasted space between the refrigerator and the wall. Build a rolling rack to slide in and out of that slot and you've got a fantastic place to store a few more jars of food. High in the kitchen and against the refrigerator can both be warm places, so try to keep these foods rotated frequently.

Dining Room

Stack boxes under the table or in unused corners of the room. Build a bench for seating at your table and store food under the bench seat.

Laundry or Utility Room

A utility room is a great place for some food storage on shelving or in cupboards. If you don't have shelving, just stack it in the room. Install cupboards or shelves above your washer and dryer to hold food in an otherwise unused space. Build a dual-purpose laundry-folding table by placing a board on top of a base made of buckets or water barrels.

Other Inside Ideas

Sturdy hanging pocket shoe organizers on the back of any door will provide a space for small items like spices, condiments, or canned goods. Look for other unused spaces like under a stairwell or up in the attic that could hold food or other preparedness supplies. Attics get warm, so they might be best for storing paper products or other items from the home, freeing up space on the main level for food. If access to your attic is difficult, install a pull-down ladder on the ceiling-mounted attic access door and you'll be more willing to use that space. Decorative baskets or bins in any room can hold food and still look classy.

Outside the House

If your property has a root cellar, use it for the fresh crops you want to store. Your canned goods can be stored in the root cellar as well. Keep them off the ground, and don't allow any jars or cans with liquid in them to freeze.

Garages and sheds offer a variety of storage options. Be aware of temperature problems, and try to store your food in the coolest part of the building. Build a loft in your garage and use it like attic space. If your food is going there, it needs to be rotated frequently. Otherwise it is an excellent place for storing all the nonfood preparedness supplies like canning supplies, extra blankets, and paper products. A camping trailer also has abundant room in it for food while it is not being used in the winter months.

Food can be kept in Mylar bags or other packaging inside of large metal drums with tight-fitting lids. The seal keeps mice and bugs out of your food. Store these drums in the shade of a carport or on the north side of the house where sun exposure will be limited. Don't label them with their contents and the neighbors will never think it's food—really, who would store their food in a barrel outside their house?

Rent a storage unit. This is one of the least convenient places to store your food and there is a cost associated with it, but it is an option for those with severe space limitations. Ask for a unit on the north side of the building or even opt for a climate-controlled storage unit to help control temperature fluctuations.

Each person's food storage inventory and home configuration will be a little different. You may need to be creative as you walk through your own home and find the spaces that can hold your food storage.

SHELVING OPTIONS

Being able to access your food makes rotation so much easier. Nothing will make you want to go out to eat faster than having to move multiple cases of food to get to the one you need for that night's meal. Shelves are a huge asset to any food storage area where you can stack food higher than two layers. So let's look at some food storage shelving options.

Flat Shelves

These shelves can be made entirely of wood or have a steel frame and wood planks. Don't go cheap here. Unless you are storing all freeze-dried strawberries, food storage is heavy. You want well-built, sturdy shelves, because the weight of buckets of wheat, bottles of peaches, and cans of green beans all add up when they're stacked on a shelf. When I was a teenager, we had cheap metal

Earthquake Proof Your Food

The shaking of an earthquake can wreak a lot of havoc in your food storage room, knocking things over, damaging cans and buckets, and breaking jars. Take steps to secure your food before an earthquake, and more of it will be intact and safe to eat afterward.

- Secure shelving units to the wall.
- Keep jars or cans in boxes.
- Use nonslip rubber lining on shelves to keep jars from sliding around.
- Block the front of the shelf with a board or bungee cord to keep items from falling off.
- Secure stacks of boxes or buckets that are more than 3-feet (1m) high.

shelves holding bottled food in my bedroom closet, and a section of those shelves decided to buckle under the weight. It was a good thing I was nearby to push them back against the wall before everything fell off, but what a mess! Don't sacrifice your investment of time and money in food to a shelf that can't handle the weight. Buy or build sturdy shelves for your food storage.

Rotation Shelves

Companies like Thrive Life offer well-designed rotation shelving in a variety of sizes for food storage cans. The sizes range from small units that sit on a shelf in your pantry up to metal freestanding units 6 feet (2 meters) high, and they can accommodate cans as small as soup cans and up to #10 cans. They are even available to fit under your bed if the bed is high enough off the ground. A less expensive option for the pantry is the cardboard can rotator from **canorganizer.com**, which is available in a number of sizes to accommodate a variety of can sizes (e.g., 10-oz. cans, 15-oz. cans, etc.) With either of these styles, cans are loaded and dispensed from the front of the shelving unit, making them excellent for stacking right against the wall.

You can also build your own rotation shelves to fit any space you have available. Basic designs are similar to flat shelving, but built with the shelves at a slight angle, with cans placed on their sides so they roll from the high side to the low side. If the shelves are wide, add dividers to keep all the cans in their own lane. Cans load in one side and dispense from the other side, so you will need access to both sides of the shelving unit. These shelves can also be built against a wall just the depth of a can (about 8 inches [20cm] deep for a #10 can, less for smaller cans) with the cans rolling along the wall rather than away from it. Another slim rotation rack design is built vertically against a wall, with cans loaded in the top and dispensed at the bottom. More advanced woodworkers can build shelves that load and dispense from the front similar to the commercial models available.

Bucket Shelves

If you want to be able to stack your buckets and still have access to what is in them, they can stack on a standard flat shelf or a specially designed bucket shelf like the one from Thrive Life. This shelving unit will hold eight 5- or 6-gallon buckets at an angle so the lids can be removed without moving the buckets at all.

Shelving makes food storage organization easier and can be the most efficient way to use open areas. Your skill level, available space, and the types of food you are storing will determine which style of shelving will work best for you.

KEEPING YOUR FOOD STORAGE ORGANIZED

Organizing your food storage helps you keep track of what you have, what you need, and where it all is. We all like to think we'll remember everything, but if food is stuffed into random places with no methodology, the chances that you'll forget what is where are greatly increased. Having an organized food storage system prevents waste, saves you time and money, and helps you keep your food storage adequately stocked so you are always ready for an emergency. There are a number of ways to organize your food storage. Choose the method that works the best for you and your personality. If you're not a meticulous person, don't use a meticulous method. Set yourself up for success by choosing a method that suits you. Use the Foods in Storage worksheet in the appendix (and downloadable from **livingreadyonline.com/foodstorage**) to keep track of where you've stored your food.

Method A: Organize by Food Type

One of the easiest methods of organizing is to keep all "like" items together in one designated location. To apply this method to food storage, sort all of your foods by category—for example, meats, vegetables, grains, sweets, dairy. Each food or category of food gets its own area, regardless of how it is preserved, so dehydrated green beans, freeze-dried green beans, home-canned green beans,

Organized food storage

and cans of green beans from the case lot sale all go together. All the spices and seasonings are in one area, all the condiments in another.

Then designate a single location for each category (such as a shelf or a set of shelves) and keep only foods that belong in that category in that location. You can use this method even if you're storing in creative spaces. For example, all the green vegetables go under Johnny's bed, and all the canned fruits go in the hall closet.

This method makes it easy to see what products you are getting low on that will need to be replenished. It also makes it quick and easy to find a specific food because there will be only one place to look for it, and putting food into storage is easy too because everything already has a designated spot.

Method B: Organize by Packaging

A second method is to organize your foods by the container they are packaged in. Buckets, cans, jars, and pouches each have their own needs in a storage area, and organizing by packaging might be the best use of your available space because same-sized items are easier to stack and reduce the amount of wasted space around them.

Method C: Organize by Meal

If you make the same types of meals regularly, you can organize your food storage by meal ingredients. So instead of spaghetti noodles being with the grains and sauce stored with canned goods, these two foods plus freeze-dried or bottled hamburger are stored near each other.

To take this one more step, place all the ingredients for one meal into a container like a paper sack and store each meal ready to grab. This system works especially well if you have set recipes for meals that you are planning to make. Separate the ingredients into individual meals and it is easy to see how many full meals you can make and if you really have all the ingredients you need.

Rotate Oldest to Newest

After you select your organizing method, be sure you remain mindful of expiration dates as you place your food in its storage location. To keep your supply of food as fresh as possible and minimize waste, it is important to eat the oldest foods first. Rotation shelves are excellent for date-based storage as the new food is conveniently loaded behind the old food. If you do not use rotation shelving, keep a permanent marker in each of your storage areas and mark foods with the date they were purchased when you add them to your storage. Then put the newest food to the back of the shelf or bottom of the stack so you use the oldest foods first.

INVENTORY

To keep track of the food you have stored, it is beneficial to have a master list and inventory. This gives you a record of the food in your storage and lets you know how much of each food item you still need to get to reach your storage goal. An inventory helps focus your purchases to those items you need most. This record is especially important when storing food in creative spaces throughout your house where it can be difficult to access or easy to forget about. The Foods in Storage worksheet in the appendix (and downloadable from **livingreadyonline.com/foodstorage**) is one way to keep an inventory. There are a variety of other methods for tracking your stored food including the old-fashioned paper and pencil, spreadsheets, online programs, and even mobile apps.

Paper and Pencil

Make a list of the foods you want and how much of them you need. Use the inventory list in the back of this book to get started. Then write down the amount of each you already have stored. If you are using creative storage spaces, also note where the items are stored. Keep the list someplace safe for adding to when you make new purchases and subtracting from when you use food from your storage. For the adding and subtracting, keep a paper and pencil or whiteboard and marker near your food storage room or in your kitchen to write on as you use food from storage. This list becomes your shopping list for replenishing your food supply and also can be used to update your master inventory list.

Spreadsheets

Inventories done with a computer spreadsheet take the paper and pencil method up a notch. Enter the items on your inventory onto lines in the first column of a spreadsheet. Use the next two columns for the total amount needed and amount on hand. With a simple equation in the fourth column, the spreadsheet can automatically determine the amount you still need to purchase. You can also add columns for package sizes, purchase price, where you purchased it, or any other information you would like.

Online Programs

Do an internet search for "online food storage inventory" and you'll get results like the Food Storage Analyzer at Emergency Essentials, and online inventory systems at **trackmyfoodstorage.com** and **stockupfood.com**. Most of these services offer free options for keeping track of your food storage online, and some have paid upgrades for more customization. These programs have many prepopulated products to choose from, the ability to add your own products, and can track expiration dates to help you use food before it expires. There are also downloadable programs for sale that perform similar functions, and all your data is stored on your own computer instead of on the internet.

Mobile Apps

Apps for Apple (iOS) and Android devices make food storage inventory detailed and quick, and as a bonus, with your inventory stored on your phone, it will be hard to lose! Look for one that allows scanning of barcodes for easy product entry. It is best if the app recognizes cans from major food storage suppliers in addition to grocery store foods. These mobile apps can alert you of upcoming expiration dates and inventory supplies in addition to food. Check the following apps:
- Prep & Pantry—iOS, Android
- Home Food Storage—iOS

- E-Food Storage—iOS, Android
- Or use a general inventory app like Inventory for Android

SECURITY

It is possible to lose all or part of your food storage either to a natural disaster or theft. One way to ensure you have food for your family is not to put all your eggs (powdered or otherwise) in one basket. Split your food storage into different areas of your home or keep some food in an alternate location. Stock each location with a variety of foods planned around meals so if that portion of your food storage were all you had, you could have more than wheat and beans on the menu.

Here are some ideas for securing portions of your food storage:
- Store some at the home of a relative or trusted friend. Offer to trade feeding them for some space in their house to store the food.
- Keep some in a hidden place in your own home—behind a false wall or in another difficult-to-find location. For those using creative spaces for storing food, this may happen without even trying!
- Cache some food in a weatherproof container either on your property or along your route to a planned evacuation location. These caches could be either hidden or buried and should also include water or a means to purify found water. Make a map or use memorable landmarks to ensure you can find your food cache when you need it.

SUMMARY

Not knowing where to put your food storage should not keep you from storing food. Consider the foods you will be storing, the space you have available, and the organization methods you want to use, then get busy putting food away to feed your family!

11. USING YOUR FOOD STORAGE

When you have even a small supply of food built up, you may want to just stand back and admire it. After all, it took a lot of planning and effort to build up that food storage! But food storage is not a museum piece. The reason you store food is not to have it sit on a shelf for the rest of your life. You store food to eat it.

TIPS FOR ROTATING

Rotation is the process of continually using the oldest food in your storage and replacing it with fresh food. By doing this, your storage is never depleted and is always as fresh as it can be. Rotation can be a little tricky, so here are some tips for successful food storage rotation.

1. **Store what you eat.** If your family will never use quinoa, don't store a bunch of it in your food storage. Be aware of allergies or food restrictions, and store the foods you will use in your regular cooking. Remember the classic food storage adage: Store what you eat and eat what you store.

2. **Know how to use what you store.** If you are storing wheat, learn how to make something you love with it. If you want to start storing a food you've never eaten before, open the first package of it and experiment with some different recipes and uses. That way you'll know if you want to purchase and store more of that food. If you do, and it becomes a regular part of your food storage, you'll be excited to use it.

3. **Date your containers.** Keep a small permanent marker near your food storage room or have one handy as you unload groceries, and write the

Shelf-Stable Substitutions

Fruits and Vegetables

Substitute fresh fruits and vegetables with home or commercially canned versions, or use dehydrated or freeze-dried or frozen versions when available.

Dairy

PERISHABLE FOOD	SHELF-STABLE SUBSTITUTION
Butter	Canned butter, butter powder (not for baking), oil
Cheese	Canned cheese, freeze-dried cheese, dry Parmesan cheese
Cream	Heavy cream powder, powdered milk
Milk	Powdered milk
Sour cream	Powdered sour cream, homemade plain yogurt
Eggs	Powdered egg, unflavored gelatin (1 tbsp. gelatin + 3 tbsp. water = 1 egg)

date on anything that is going in the food storage. Usually the month and year are sufficient. You could also use your marker to circle the printed expiration dates.

4. **Use rotation shelving.** We covered rotation shelving in depth in chapter ten. Load new food in one side and pull from the other side and you'll always get the oldest cans first.

5. **Perform periodic rotation maintenance.** Reorganize your food storage areas every shopping trip, every six months, or just after major purchases. Move older items to the front and put newer foods behind or in the areas that are difficult to reach. Spending time getting to the back corners of your food storage room also lets you do a deep clean of the storage areas and will reveal any sign of pests.

6. **Use a food storage tracking program** or app like Prep & Pantry that alerts you of upcoming expiration dates in your stored food.

Meat

PERISHABLE FOOD	SHELF-STABLE SUBSTITUTION
Bacon	Canned bacon, TVP* bacon bits
Beef	Home or commercially canned beef, freeze-dried beef chunks
Chicken	Home or commercially canned chicken, freeze-dried chicken, chicken TVP
Fish	Canned tuna, canned salmon, freeze-dried salmon
Ground beef	Home-canned ground beef, freeze-dried ground beef
Ham	Freeze-dried ham, ham TVP, bacon bits, canned ham
Pork	Home or commercially canned pork
Sausage	Freeze-dried sausage, sausage TVP

TVP is an acronym for textured vegetable protein, also occasionally called textured soy protein (TSP) or soy meat.

There is no finish line with food storage. You don't reach a point and declare yourself the winner. In a good food storage plan, food is constantly being used and replaced. If it is not rotated, you can end up with foods that you cannot use. Rotating your food storage will prevent waste and keep your supply of food storage as fresh as possible, ensuring that you have food ready to be eaten when you need it.

COOKING WITH FOOD STORAGE

Don't be afraid of using food storage in your cooking. With a little practice, you'll be making dinner from shelf-stable foods on a regular basis. Here are some general tips to get you started:

1. When substituting canned foods for fresh, drain the liquid from the cans prior to use.
2. Canned foods are already cooked, so their cooking times are less than that of fresh foods.

Expiration Dates and Bad Food

Expiration dates stamped on canned foods are not some magical date that your food suddenly isn't safe to eat anymore. Best by and sell by dates are guidelines for peak food freshness, but food has been shown to stay good long past the stamped expiration date. However, most food does eventually go bad. Here's how to identify food that should not be consumed:

- can or lid is bulging, or excessive pressure is released when can is opened
- seal is broken
- can shows signs of corrosion
- food seeping from can seals
- food looks bad, moldy, or cloudy
- food smells bad after opening
- visual signs of insect infestation in dry foods like webbing, larva, or exoskeleton debris

If your food is not edible, all is not lost. Use it to feed animals like chickens or pigs, or if it is not greasy, add it to a compost pile to enrich your gardening soil.

3. When substituting dehydrated foods for fresh, remember dehydrated foods are smaller than their fresh counterparts. Refer to the Dry to Fresh Conversion Table in the appendix for help converting measurements when using dehydrated foods. Dehydrated foods will need to cook for twenty minutes or longer with ample liquid to fully reconstitute.

4. When substituting freeze-dried foods for fresh, the flavor and texture will be similar to using frozen substitutes. Most freeze-dried foods reconstitute very quickly in either warm or cold water.

5. When substituting powdered foods for liquids such as milk, tomato sauce, and sour cream, reconstitute the powder into liquid form prior to use in the recipe. If used in baking, the dry powder can be mixed in with the other dry ingredients as long as you increase the amount of liquid required for the recipe by the amount that would have been used to reconstitute the powdered food. Refer to the Dry to Fresh Conversion Table for mixing ratios for powdered products.

CONVERTING RECIPES

Almost any recipe can be made food storage friendly by substituting shelf-stable foods for the perishable fresh items in the recipe. The end result is your very own food storage recipe collection made from meals your family already eats.

See the Shelf-Stable Substitutions sidebar for a list of the more common shelf-stable substitutions. Here's how to use the substitutions to make your own favorite recipes into shelf-stable food storage recipes.

1. **Start with a recipe.** Most recipes can be converted to food storage, but some, like a fresh green salad, won't work with only shelf-stable ingredients.

2. **Identify the perishable ingredients.** Anything that requires refrigeration or doesn't store well will need to be replaced with a shelf-stable alternative.

3. **Determine the best shelf-stable substitute.** Some things can be substituted very easily; other items you may need to substitute with something similar. Minor ingredients can be omitted from the recipe if there is no good alternative. If a primary ingredient cannot be substituted, you may need to choose another recipe to convert. Calculate measures of shelf-stable products and extra water requirements if necessary. If using dehydrated or powered substitutes, refer to the Dry to Fresh Conversion Table in the appendix for measurements.

4. **Test it out.** It may not work perfectly the first time and will usually taste a little different than the original. Make any adjustments to the recipe and save it to use in your food storage plan.

To see how food storage recipe conversion works, let's convert a couple of recipes together. We'll start with a soup and then make a casserole food storage friendly.

Clam Chowder Soup Recipe Conversion

Soups are one of the easiest recipes to convert to shelf-stable food storage recipes. The recipes already plan for foods to be boiling in water, so swapping dried foods for fresh might change the amount of liquid required, but doesn't change the cooking process much. Here's how to convert a recipe:

1. **Start with a recipe.** For this example, we'll use Grandma Paskett's Clam Chowder recipe found in the sidebar.

2. **Identify the perishable ingredients**. In this recipe, the following ingredients are not shelf-stable: potatoes, celery, carrot, onion, butter, milk.

3. **Determine the best shelf-stable substitutions.** Most foods in this recipe have dehydrated or freeze-dried options. Freeze-dried foods

Grandma Paskett's Clam Chowder

Ingredients

2 large potatoes diced
2 stalks celery diced
1 large carrot grated
1 onion diced
2 cans clams
½ tsp. thyme
1 tsp. salt
Pepper to taste

White Sauce

¾ cup butter
½ cup flour
3 cups milk

Instructions

1. Cook vegetables in a pot with enough water to cover them plus the juice from the clam cans.
2. Make white sauce by heating butter, stirring in flour, adding milk, and heating until thick. Add white sauce to the vegetables. Add clams and seasonings.

reconstitute faster than dehydrated foods, so the soup will need to boil longer if you choose to use dehydrated foods. Amounts of dried foods to use for substituting are estimates.

- **Potatoes.** The potatoes in the recipe are diced, so use either dehydrated or freeze-dried diced potatoes. You'll get approximately 3 cups of potato dices from those two large potatoes and that will be equal to about 3 cups of freeze-dried potato dices or 1½ cups of dehydrated potato dices. If you only have shreds or slices, those can be used as well, just break the slices into smaller pieces before cooking.
- **Celery.** Two stalks of celery equal about 1 cup of diced celery. Substitute 1 cup of freeze-dried celery or ¼ cup of dehydrated celery.
- **Carrot.** One large carrot is approximately ½ cup shredded carrot. There are not freeze-dried carrots they don't like the freeze-drying process and turn white—so we'll substitute about ¼ cup dehydrated carrots. Unless you dehydrated your own shredded carrot, your dehydrated carrots are probably diced. You could

Shelf-Stable Clam Chowder Conversion

Ingredients

1½ cups dehydrated
    potato dices
¼ cup dehydrated celery
¼ cup dehydrated carrot
3 tbsp. dried onion
2 cans clams
½ tsp. thyme
1 tsp. salt
Pepper to taste

White Sauce

¾ cup oil
½ cup flour
½ cup butter powder (optional)
9 tbsp. powdered milk plus
    3 cups water

Instructions

1. Cook vegetables in a pot with twice as much water as vegetables plus the juice from the clam cans. Cook until tender adding more water as needed.
2. Make white sauce by heating oil, stirring in flour, adding milk powder, optional butter powder, and water (may need to be whisked) and heating until thick. Add white sauce to the vegetables. Add clams and seasonings.

run these through a blender to break them up or just use them as carrot dices in your soup instead of shreds.

- **Onion.** One medium onion is about ⅔ cup chopped onion. Substitute with approximately ⅔ cup freeze-dried onion, 3 tablespoons dried onion, or 2 teaspoons onion powder.
- **Butter.** The butter is used as fat for making a sauce, so powdered butter, which does not melt, won't work as a substitute. Replace the butter with an oil and add butter powder to the soup for flavoring if desired.
- **Milk.** The powdered milk in my cupboard is an instant milk that calls for 3 tablespoons per cup, but be sure to check your can for mixing instructions—powdered milk has one of the widest variances in mixing ratios between brands of any dried

Turkey Tetrazzini Casserole

Ingredients

8 oz. spaghetti, broken into bite-
sized pieces
5 tbsp. butter
6 tbsp. flour
3 cups chicken broth
1 cup cream
1 tsp. salt

Pepper to taste
1 cup mushrooms
½ cup green pepper
3 cups cooked turkey
½ cup Parmesan cheese
½ cup cheddar cheese

Instructions

1. Cook spaghetti in boiling water per instructions on box.
2. In a skillet, melt butter and blend in flour. Stir in broth and add cream. Cook until thickened.
3. Add salt, pepper, cooked spaghetti, mushrooms, peppers, and turkey and heat through.
4. Put entire contents of skillet into a 9" × 13" (23cm × 33cm) pan and sprinkle the top with cheeses. Bake at 350°F (177°C) for thirty minutes.

food. With my milk it will take 9 tablespoons of milk and 3 cups of water to substitute for 3 cups of milk.

With the substitutions, here is the new food storage friendly clam chowder recipe, found in the Shelf-Stable Clam Chowder Conversion sidebar. Be sure to test the converted recipe to make sure you like the results. If you find areas that don't work well as you cook or substitutions that needed more or less dried product, make a note for the next time you make that recipe.

Turkey Tetrazzini Casserole Recipe Conversion

Now let's convert a casserole recipe. Using the conversion steps again, start with a recipe. We'll use one of my family's favorite recipes for Turkey Tetrazzini Casserole (see sidebar).

In this recipe, the following ingredients are not shelf-stable and need an appropriate substitute: butter, cream, mushrooms, green pepper, cooked turkey, cheddar cheese. Chicken broth (canned) and Parmesan cheese have shelf lives of less than three years and could also be substituted.

Shelf-Stable Turkey Tetrazzini Casserole

Ingredients

8 oz. spaghetti, broken up into bite-sized pieces
5 tbsp. oil
3–4 tbsp. butter powder (optional)
6 tbsp. flour
3 cups chicken broth or 3 tsp. bouillon plus 3 cups water
4 tbsp. powdered milk plus 1 cup water
1 tsp. salt
Pepper to taste
1 cup freeze-dried mushrooms
½ cup freeze-dried green pepper
3 cups freeze-dried turkey chunks
½ cup Parmesan cheese
½ cup freeze-dried cheddar cheese

Instructions

1. Cook spaghetti in boiling water per the instructions on the box.
2. In a dish, reconstitute mushrooms, peppers, and turkey, draining any excess water.
3. In a separate dish, reconstitute freeze-dried cheddar cheese, draining any excess water.
4. In a skillet, heat oil and blend in flour. Stir in broth (or water and bouillon) and add powdered milk and water (may need to whisk it in). Cook until thickened.
5. Add salt, pepper, cooked spaghetti, reconstituted mushrooms, peppers, and turkey to thickened broth and heat through.
6. Put into a 9" × 13" (23cm × 33cm) pan and sprinkle the top with cheeses. Bake at 350°F (177°C) for thirty minutes.

Now determine the best shelf-stable substitutions.

- **Butter.** This butter is being used as a fat for thickening the sauce, so powdered butter, which does not melt, won't work as a substitution. Substitute a shelf-stable oil like vegetable oil or coconut oil. Butter powder can be added to the sauce for flavoring if desired.

- **Cream.** Heavy cream powder or powdered milk can both be used. Powdered milk is more common and has a longer shelf life. Mix the powdered milk at a higher powder-to-water ratio than normal to substitute for cream. The powdered milk I'm using is an instant milk that calls for 3 tablespoons per cup. Raise the amount to 4 or 5 tablespoons to mix a cup of cream.
- **Mushrooms.** One 8-oz. can of mushrooms is around a cup. Or use 1 cup freeze-dried mushrooms or about ½ cup dehydrated mushrooms. Because this is not a soup that will boil with plenty of liquid for fifteen minutes or more, rehydrate the freeze-dried or dehydrated mushrooms before adding them.
- **Green pepper.** Substitute with either ½ cup freeze-dried or ¼ cup dehydrated green pepper. Boiling the dehydrated peppers prior to adding them will tenderize them and keep them from being tough.
- **Cooked turkey.** Use 3 cups of freeze-dried turkey or freeze-dried chicken, or 1 cup chicken TVP. Reconstitute either before adding them to a casserole recipe.
- **Cheddar cheese.** The cheese in this recipe is melted on the top, so a cheese powder won't work. Use ½ cup shredded canned cheese or rehydrate ½ cup of freeze-dried cheddar cheese.
- **Broth.** Use cans or mix using bouillon powder or cubes. Add 1 teaspoon powder or 1 bouillon cube to 1 cup of water to make a cup of broth. This recipe would need 3 teaspoons bouillon powder or 3 bouillon cubes plus 3 cups of water.
- **Parmesan cheese.** If you need to substitute this, use additional freeze-dried or canned cheese or omit from the recipe.

These substitutions are reflected in the Shelf-Stable Turkey Tetrazzini Casserole sidebar. Cook the new recipe and make sure it works for you. Note any adjustments in amounts or cooking methods for the next time.

Now you should be ready to tackle one of your own favorite recipes. Using your food storage to cook recipes your family already loves helps you know which foods to store and how to use them. Plus you'll have a little less palate shock if you ever need to use your food storage exclusively.

POWERLESS COOKING METHODS

Many emergency situations will result in the loss of electricity. The majority of your food storage still needs to be cooked. Making a plan for cooking without electricity will help ensure you're not eating all your food storage cold and raw. So here are some options for cooking when there is no electricity.

EcoZoom Versa rocket stove

Sun Oven solar cooker

1. **Fire.** Build a fire in a fire pit, barrel, or other enclosure so you don't add an uncontrolled fire to your emergency! Do not cook your food over fuel that produces toxic fumes as it burns like tires or carpet. Roast your food on a stick, or use a metal grate or tripod over your fire and cook in sturdy pots and pans.

2. **Wood or coal stove.** The flat top of a wood or coal stove can be used to cook like a range. An antique wood-burning kitchen stove would be ideal, but a stove built to heat a home with a flat top would work as well. Cooking on a wood stove will serve the dual purpose of heating your home as well—perfect for a winter emergency.

3. **Rocket stove.** Rocket stoves are designed to burn biomass fuel like sticks, but use less of it than an open fire. You can make your own rocket stove, or purchase one like the EcoZoom stove. Volcano Stoves use a similar fuel-conserving design as a rocket stove and are also available with a propane adaptor for an additional fuel option.

4. **A barbecue grill.** An outdoor grill, either gas or charcoal, is a simple powerless cooking option many of us already use regularly. But it's not just for steaks and burgers. Any food small enough to fall through the grate can be cooked in foil or a pan over the heat source.

5. **Camping stove.** With styles ranging from pocket-sized backpacking stoves to briefcase-style double burner stoves, there's surely one of these portable stoves that will fit your needs for preparedness and maybe even make itself a regular participant on your camping trips as well. Larger camping stoves, like those built by Camp Chef, use the same propane tanks as a gas grill, increasing your cooking options with

the same fuel you may already have on hand. Each of these camping stoves uses a specific fuel, so be sure you have sufficient fuel stored to be able to use your stove when you need it.

6. **Gas range.** If you have a gas range in your kitchen and the gas lines are not damaged, you can use that range in your home for cooking. Just bypass the electronic ignition and light it with a match or other fire starter. A gas oven will not work without power, only the stove top.

7. **Solar oven.** Make a solar oven or purchase one like the All American Sun Oven. Solar ovens magnify the heat from the sun and work on sunny days in any season. In winter months, your best cooking time is between 10 A.M. and 2 P.M., so plan your meals accordingly. A solar oven can cook anything you'd put in your normal oven and can also be used to dehydrate foods and pasteurize water.

8. **WonderBox or HayBox.** After food has reach the correct temperature or water has been brought to a boil with one of the previous cooking methods, placing the pot into one of these insulated containers allows the food to continue cooking without using additional fuel.

Having alternate methods of cooking the food you have stored will give you the ability to have a hot meal even when the power is out. And I don't know about you, but for me a hot meal beats cold soup in a can any day.

SUMMARY

Throughout this book, we have covered many options for storing food. Remember, food storage is not one-size-fits-all. Each of us is in a different situation. Some live in an apartment in the city, some in a big house in the country, and most of us live somewhere in between. We are young, not-so-young, single, married, or have families or friends we want to take care of. With the information you are holding in your hand, I believe each of you can make wise choices to provide food for your own family, allowing you to be more self-reliant and prepared for whatever lies ahead.

APPENDIX

This appendix includes the worksheets mentioned throughout the book. Photocopy them for your personal use, or download the worksheets for free from **www.livingreadyonline/foodstorage** and print as many copies as you need for personal use.

Menu Method Planning Sheet

Recipe name: _____

Number of servings in single batch:_____

Number of times recipe will be served: _____

SINGLE BATCH QUANTITY X NUMBER OF TIMES RECIPE WILL BE SERVED	QUANTITY USED TO MAKE A SINGLE BATCH	INGREDIENT

Download a printable version of this worksheet at
www.livingreadyonline.com/foodstorage

Food Inventory List

Download a printable version of this worksheet at
www.livingreadyonline.com/foodstorage

Date of Inventory:_____

Food Quickly Eaten

FOOD	NUMBER CONSUMED IN 1 MONTH (USE TALLY MARKS)	NUMBER NEEDED (3-MONTH SUPPLY)

Multi-Use Food (e.g., condiments, spices)

FOOD	DATE FOOD WAS OPENED	DATE FOOD WAS USED UP	NUMBER NEEDED (3-MONTH SUPPLY)

Master Menu List

Download a printable version of this worksheet at
www.livingreadyonline.com/foodstorage

Breakfast

NUMBER OF TIMES RECIPE WILL BE USED	RECIPE

Total: _____ days of breakfast

Lunch

NUMBER OF TIMES RECIPE WILL BE USED	RECIPE

Total: _____ days of lunch

Master Menu List

continued

Dinner

NUMBER OF TIMES RECIPE WILL BE USED	RECIPE

Total: ____ days of dinner

Master Menu List

continued

Sides

Some dinner recipes won't require any side dishes, while others will need sides to balance the nutrition, add variety and provide enough calories. Think about what sides you normally serve with each main dish and plan accordingly.

Vegetables

NUMBER OF TIMES SIDE WILL BE USED	VEGETABLES

Total: _____ days of vegetables

Fruit (Canned)

NUMBER OF TIMES SIDE WILL BE USED	FRUIT

Total: ____ days of fruit

Master Menu List

continued

Grains

NUMBER OF TIMES SIDE WILL BE USED	GRAIN

Total: _____ days of grains

Potatoes

NUMBER OF TIMES SIDE WILL BE USED	POTATO

Total: _____ days of potatoes

Snacks

NUMBER OF TIMES SNACK WILL BE USED	SNACK

Total: _____ days of snacks

APPENDIX

One Year of Food Chart

Download a printable version of this worksheet at
www.livingreadyonline.com/foodstorage

Multiply the number of people in your family by the
suggested food storage amount for an individual to
determine how much food your entire family needs
for one year. Number of people: _____

Grains (rice, pasta, flour, cereal, wheat, oats):   300 lbs. × _____ = _____ lbs.

Legumes (beans, lentils):   60 lbs. × _____ = _____ lbs.

Fats and oils (cooking oil, shortening):   25 lbs. × _____ = _____ lbs.

Dairy (powdered milk, evaporated milk, cheeses):   75 lbs. × _____ = _____ lbs.

Sugars (sugar, brown and powdered sugar,
honey, drink mixes, jams and jellies):   60 lbs. × _____ = _____ lbs.

Fruits (canned, dried, juices):   185 lbs. × _____ = _____ lbs.

Vegetables (canned, dried):   185 lbs. × _____ = _____ lbs.

Baking powder: 1 lb. × _____ = _____ lbs.

Baking soda: 1 lb. × _____ = _____ lbs.

Vinegar: ½ gal. × _____ = _____ gal.

Yeast: ½ lb. × _____ = _____ lbs.

Salt: 5 lbs. × _____ = _____ lbs.

Additional needs: _____

_____

_____

_____

_____

_____

Adapted from the Church of Jesus Christ of Latter-day Saints' *Essentials of Home Production & Storage* book.

Foods in Storage

Download a printable version of this worksheet at
www.livingreadyonline.com/foodstorage

FOOD	AMOUNT	LOCATION OF STORAGE	DATE STORED	ROTATION DATE

My Family's Dietary Needs and Preferences

Download a printable version of this worksheet at
www.livingreadyonline.com/foodstorage

Preferred types of protein _____

_____

Quantity needed _____

How it is best stored_____

_____

Preferred types of dairy _____

_____

Quantity needed _____

How it is best stored_____

_____

Preferred types of fruits _____

_____

Quantity needed _____

How it is best stored_____

_____

Preferred types of vegetables _____

_____

Quantity needed _____

How it is best stored_____

_____

My Family's Dietary Needs and Preferences

continued

Preferred types of grains _____

_____

Quantity needed _____

How it is best stored_____

_____

Preferred types of oils_____

_____

Quantity needed _____

How it is best stored_____

_____

Preferred types of seasonings _____

_____

Quantity needed _____

How it is best stored_____

_____

Preferred types of sweets _____

_____

Quantity needed _____

How it is best stored_____

_____

Any dietary restrictions/considerations (including dislikes of certain family members)

_____

Food Storage Location

Download a printable version of this worksheet at
www.livingreadyonline.com/foodstorage

Use this worksheet to help you carve out space on your property for your food storage.

Possible Food Storage Location _____

How Much Food Will Fit There

_____

_____

_____

_____

_____

Type of Food Storage Best Suited for This Location

_____

_____

_____

_____

_____

Steps That Need to Be Taken to Get It Ready

_____

_____

_____

_____

_____

Savings Through Sacrifice Worksheet

Use this worksheet to help keep track of funds you can use for food storage purchases instead of other items. Be very diligent about recording the money you save when you make a conscious effort to forgo something with the intention of saving for food storage.

Money Needed for Food Storage Purchases: _____

Item or Service Not Purchased   Savings Earned

_____   _____

_____   _____

_____   _____

_____   _____

_____   _____

_____   _____

_____   _____

_____   _____

_____   _____

_____   _____

_____   _____

_____   _____

_____   _____

_____   _____

_____   _____

_____   _____

_____   _____

_____   _____

                                              TOTAL: _____

Dry to Fresh Conversion Table

Dehydrated Foods

Soak dry product in water for four to six hours or cook in water for twenty to thirty minutes.

PRODUCT	FRESH	DRY	WATER
Broccoli	1 cup	½ cup	1 cup
Carrots	1 cup	½ cup	1 cup
Celery	1 cup	½ cup	1 cup
Corn	1 cup	½ cup	1½ cups
Green beans	1 cup	½ cup	1 cup
Mushrooms	1 cup	1 cup	2 cups
Onions	1 cup	⅓ cup	1 cup
Peas	1 cup	⅓ cup	1 cup
Peppers	1 cup	½ cup	1 cup
Potatoes, diced or shredded	1 cup	½ cup	1½ cups
Spinach	1 cup	1 cup	1½ cups

Powdered Foods

These amounts are a general rule and can vary between brands. Always check the package for mixing instructions if available.

POWDERED PRODUCT	FRESH	POWDER	WATER
Butter	1 cup	1 cup	⅓ cup
Cheese sauce	1 cup	¼ cup	1 cup, hot
Milk	1 cup	3 Tablespoon	1 cup
Shortening	1 cup	1 cup	¼ cup
Sour cream	1 cup	1 cup	¼ cup
Tomato paste from powder	1 cup	½ cup	1 cup
Tomato sauce from powder	1 cup	⅓ cup	1 cup

Freeze-Dried Foods

Reconstitute using the same amount dry as fresh with enough water to cover the dry product. Most are fully hydrated in one to three minutes and do not require heating.

Food Storage Purchasing Checklist

Grains (approx. 25 pounds [11kg] per person per month)
- six-grain cereal
- nine-grain cereal
- amaranth
- barley
- corn meal
- farina/germade
- flour
- oat groats, whole
- oats, instant
- pancake mix
- pasta: egg noodles
- pasta: spaghetti
- pasta: macaroni
- pasta: other
- quinoa
- rice, brown
- rice, white
- rice, instant
- spelt
- wheat, white
- wheat, red

Dairy (approx. 6 pounds [3kg] per person per month)
- instant milk
- non-instant milk
- cheese powder
- cheese, canned
- cheese, freeze-dried
- buttermilk powder
- sour cream powder
- yogurt, dry culture
- yogurt, freeze-dried

Legumes (approx. 5 pounds [2kg] per person per month)
- black beans
- kidney beans
- lentils
- lima beans
- mung beans
- navy beans
- pink beans
- pinto beans
- red beans
- split peas

Other Protein (as desired)
- canned meat: tuna
- canned meat: wild game
- canned meat: other
- freeze-dried meat: beef
- freeze-dried meat: chicken
- freeze-dried meat: ham
- freeze-dried meat: other
- textured vegetable protein (TVP)

- powdered eggs
- peanut butter

Fruits (approx. 15 pounds [7kg] per person per month)
- canned peaches
- canned pears
- canned mandarin oranges
- canned pineapple
- canned mixed fruit
- freeze-dried apples
- freeze-dried berries
- freeze-dried pineapple
- freeze-dried peaches
- dehydrated apples
- raisins
- other dried fruits

Vegetables (approx. 15 pounds [7kg] per person per month)
- canned beans
- canned corn
- canned mixed vegetables
- canned peas
- canned spinach
- canned tomato products
- other canned vegetables
- dehydrated beans
- dehydrated broccoli
- dehydrated carrots
- dehydrated corn
- dehydrated onions
- dehydrated potatoes (flakes, dices, powdered)
- other dehydrated vegetables
- freeze-dried beans
- freeze-dried corn
- freeze-dried peas
- freeze-dried peppers

- other freeze-dried vegetables
- tomato powder

Fats (approx. 2 pounds [907g] per person per month)
- coconut oil
- olive or vegetable oil
- shortening
- other oil
- butter powder
- shortening powder

Sugars (approx. 5 pounds [2kg] per person per month)
- brown sugar
- powdered sugar
- white sugar
- honey
- corn syrup
- maple syrup
- molasses
- jam and jelly
- drink mixes

Baking Needs (as desired)
- baking powder
- baking soda
- cocoa powder
- cornstarch
- unflavored gelatin
- yeast

Spices and Flavorings (as desired)
- basil
- bouillon: beef
- bouillon: chicken
- chili powder
- cilantro
- cinnamon

- cumin
- dill seed
- extract: almond
- extract: mint
- extract: vanilla
- garlic powder
- ginger
- Italian seasoning
- lemon pepper
- mustard: dry
- onion powder
- oregano
- paprika
- parsley flakes
- pepper
- sage
- salt: canning
- salt: iodized
- seasoned salt
- thyme
- vinegar
- other spices and flavorings

Condiments (as desired)
- barbecue sauce
- ketchup
- mayonnaise
- mustard
- olives
- peppers: banana

- peppers: hot
- pickles
- relish
- salad dressing
- salsa
- soy sauce
- teriyaki sauce

Convenience Meals
- canned soups
- canned pasta
- canned chili
- boxed pasta or rice meals
- freeze-dried or dehydrated meals
- MREs

Garden Seeds
- non-hybrid (also called open-pollinated or heirloom) seeds suited to your region's growing conditions

Sources for Food Storage

Augason Farms
1911 South 3850 West
Salt Lake City, UT 84104
800-878-0099
augasonfarms.com

Honeyville Grain
1080 North Main Suite 101
Brigham City, UT 84302
888-810-3212
honeyville.com

Emergency Essentials
653 North 1500 West
Orem, UT 84057
800-999-1863
beprepared.com

Food Insurance
695 North Kay's Drive Suite 7b
Kaysville, UT 84037
866-946-8366
foodinsurance.com

Nitro-Pak Preparedness Center
375 West 910 South
Heber City, UT 84032
800-866-4876
nitro-pak.com

Ready Made Resources
239 Cagle Road
Tellico Plains, TN 37385
800-627-3809
readymaderesources.com

The Ready Store
14015 S Minuteman Drive
Draper, UT 84020
800-773-5331
www.thereadystore.com

Thrive Life*
691 S Auto Mall Dr.
American Fork, UT 84003
877-743-5373
foodstoragefun.thrivelife.com/home
*The author has an affiliate relationship with Thrive Life and may receive compensation if you make a purchase through this link.

Food Storage Tools You May Need

For Food Preservation

- water bath canner
- pressure canner
- canning jars
- two-piece caps
- Tattler reusable canning lids
- jar funnel
- jar lifter tongs
- dehydrator (electric or solar)

For Packaging Food

- #10 can sealer
- heat sealer for Mylar bags
- vacuum sealer
- jar sealer attachment for vacuum sealer

For Emergency Food Preparation

- manual can opener
- bucket opener
- water filter
- powerless cooker
- sturdy pans and utensils that can cook over high heat

Other Emergency Supplies for Your Home

Although the focus of this book is food for preparedness, food is not all you'll want to be able to provide for your family in an emergency. The following are some nonfood categories you'll also want to prepare for, including suggestions for some items in each category. Adapt or expand this list to fit your individual needs.

- **Medical Supplies:** First aid kit, bandages, pain relievers, cough and cold medication, anti-diarrheal medication, hydrogen peroxide, rubbing alcohol, children's medications, extra prescription medication if possible, ointments, thermometer
- **Sanitation:** Cleaning products, vinegar, emergency toilet, hand sanitizer, bleach
- **Personal Hygiene:** Toothbrushes, toothpaste, soap, shampoo, deodorant, feminine hygiene, lotion, lip balm, sunblock, insect repellent
- **Paper Products:** Plates, napkins, paper towels, cutlery, zip-seal bags, aluminum foil
- **Laundry Supplies:** Laundry soap, large tub for washing, clothesline, clothespins
- **Shelter and Bedding:** Tent, plastic sheeting, duct tape, sleeping bags, blankets, sheets, pillowcases, cots
- **Clothes and Shoes:** Winter clothing—coats, hats, gloves, boots, snow pants; sturdy shoes; clothes and shoes for children in sizes larger than they currently wear
- **Sewing:** Lightweight and heavy fabric, needles, thread, scissors, buttons, safety pins
- **Communication:** Battery-powered radio, CB radio, handheld walkie-talkies, HAM radio (if licensed)
- **Hand Tools:** Hammer, saw, wrenches, screwdrivers, pliers, crowbar, shovel, rakes, axe
- **Light and Heat:** Flashlights, oil lamps, candles, solar lights, light sticks, hand warmers, fire starters, wood-burning stove, kerosene heater
- **Fuel and Power:** Stabilized fuel, wood, propane tanks, solar battery charger, rechargeable batteries, generator
- **Vital Records** (hard copy and digital copies): Birth certificate, Social Security card, passport, driver's license, firearm permit, marriage certificate, family photos, insurance policies, mortgage/deed, vehicle titles

- **Baby Supplies:** Diapers (cloth or lots of disposable), wipes, clothes, medication, formula, bottles, baby food grinder
- **Pet Supplies:** Food, leashes, kennel, vaccination record, medications
- **Security:** Extra door locks, fencing, alarms, self-defense training, firearms and ammunition

Food Storage Blogs

Food Storage and Survival: **foodstorageandsurvival.com**

Chef Tess Bakeresse: **cheftessbakeresse.blogspot.com**

Dehydrate 2 Store: **dehydrate2store.com**

Everyday Food Storage: **everydayfoodstorage.net**

Food Storage Made Easy: **foodstoragemadeeasy.net**

Food Storage Moms: **www.foodstoragemoms.com**

Game & Garden: **gameandgarden.com**

My Food Storage Cookbook: **myfoodstoragecookbook.com**

Ready Nutrition: **readynutrition.com**

Simply Canning: **simplycanning.com**

General Preparedness Blogs

American Preppers Network: **americanpreppersnetwork.com**

Are We Crazy, or What?: **arewecrazyorwhat.net**

Backdoor Survival: **www.backdoorsurvival.com**

Common Sense Homesteading: **www.commonsensehome.com**

Mom With a Prep: **momwithaprep.com**

Prepared Housewives: **prepared-housewives.com**

Reality Survival: **realitysurvival.com**

Survival Common Sense: **survivalcommonsense.com**

The Survival Mom: **thesurvivalmom.com**

Willow Haven Outdoor: **willowhavenoutdoor.com**

INDEX

To my husband and children

ACKNOWLEDGMENTS

Heartfelt thanks to my family and my mom for always supporting and believing in me, my fabulous friend Dianna for reminding me of what I learned in college English class, my sweet Sharla for asking for help, my editors Jackie and Michelle for all their work getting this project finished, and my Father in Heaven for blessing me in more ways than I can number.

ABOUT THE AUTHOR

Angela Paskett writes the blog Food Storage and Survival, **foodstorageandsurvival. com**, and hosts the weekly Food Storage and Survival Radio Show focusing on family preparedness. She has been actively storing and eating food with her family for over fifteen years. She teaches workshops on family preparedness and storing and preserving food to anyone who will listen, including preparedness fairs, civic groups, churches, and online. Angela is a member of the Church of Jesus Christ of Latter-day Saints and lives in rural Utah with her husband, four children, an animal menagerie, garden, and food storage.

An imprint of Penguin Random House LLC

penguinrandomhouse.com

ISBN 978-1-4403-3353-8

Printed in the United States of America

12th Printing

Edited by Jacqueline Musser and Michelle Ehrhard
Designed by Clare Finney